EDGAR CAYCE ON
REINCARNATION

The truth about people who have lived more than once
— and what it means for you

EDGAR CAYCE ON REINCARNATION

NOEL LANGLEY

Edited by HUGH LYNN CAYCE

Aquarian/Thorsons

An Imprint of HarperCollins*Publishers*

The Aquarian Press
An Imprint of HarperCollins*Publishers*
77–85 Fulham Palace Road,
Hammersmith, London W6 8JB

First UK edition 1989
This edition published by arrangement
with Warner Books, Inc., New York
3 5 7 9 10 8 6 4

© The Association for Research and
Enlightenment, Inc. 1967

Noel Langley asserts the moral right to
be identified as the author of this work

A catalogue record for this book
is available from the British Library

ISBN 1 85030 857 7

Printed in Great Britain by
HarperCollinsManufacturing Glasgow

Contents

FOREWORD

WHO WAS EDGAR CAYCE?

The six books which have been written about Edgar Cayce have totaled more than a million in sales. More than ten other books have devoted sections to his life and talents. He has been featured in dozens of magazines and hundreds of newspaper articles dating from 1900 to the present. What was so unique about him?

It depends on through whose eyes you look at him. A goodly number of his contemporaries knew the "waking" Edgar Cayce as a gifted professional photographer. Another group (predominantly children) admired him as a warm and friendly Sunday School teacher. His own family knew him as a wonderful husband and father.

The "sleeping" Edgar Cayce was an entirely different figure—a psychic known to thousands of people, in all walks of life, who had cause to be grateful for his help. Indeed, many of them believed that he alone had either "saved" or "changed" their lives when all seemed lost. The "sleeping" Edgar Cayce was a medical diagnostician, a prophet, and a devoted proponent of Bible lore.

In June, 1954, the University of Chicago held him in sufficient respect to accept a Ph.D. thesis based on a study of his life and work. In this thesis the writer referred to him as a "religious seer." In that same year, the children's comic book *House of Mystery*

7

bestowed on him the impressive title of "America's Most Mysterious Man"!

Even as a child, on a farm near Hopkinsville, Kentucky, where he was born on March 18, 1877, Edgar Cayce displayed powers of perception which seemed to extend beyond the normal range of the five senses. At the age of six or seven he told his parents that he was able to see and talk to "visions," sometimes of relatives who had recently died. His parents attributed this to the overactive imagination of a lonely child who had been influenced by the dramatic language of the revival meetings which were popular in that section of the country. Later, by sleeping with his head on his schoolbooks, he developed some form of photographic memory which helped him advance rapidly in the country school. This gift faded, however, and Edgar was only able to complete his seventh grade before he had to seek his own place in the world.

By the age of twenty-one he had become the salesman for a wholesale stationery company. At this time he developed a gradual paralysis of the throat muscles which threatened the loss of his voice. When doctors were unable to find a physical cause for this condition, hypnosis was tried, but failed to have any permanent effect. As a last resort, Edgar asked a friend to help him re-enter the same kind of hypnotic sleep that had enabled him to memorize his schoolbooks as a child. His friend gave him the necessary suggestion, and once he was in a self-induced trance, Edgar came to grips with his own problem. He recommended medication and manipulative therapy which successfully restored his voice and repaired his system.

A group of physicians from Hopkinsville and Bowling Green, Kentucky, took advantage of his unique talent to diagnose their own patients. They soon discovered that Cayce only needed to be given the name and address of a patient, wherever he was, to be able to "tune in" telepathically on that individual's mind and body as easily as if they were both in the same room. He needed, and was given, no other information regarding any patient.

One of the young M.D.'s, Dr. Wesley Ketchum, submitted a report on this unorthodox procedure to a clinical research society in Boston. On the ninth of October, 1910, *The New York Times* carried two pages of headlines and pictures. From that day on, troubled people from all over the country sought the "wonder man's" help.

When Edgar Cayce died on January 3, 1945, in Virginia Beach, Virginia, he left well over 14,000 documented stenographic records of the telepathic-clairvoyant statements he had given for more than six thousand different people over a period of forty-three years. These documents are referred to as "Readings."

The Readings constitute one of the largest and most impressive records of psychic perception ever to emanate from a single individual. Together with their relevant records, correspondence and reports, they have been cross-indexed under thousands of subject headings and placed at the disposal of psychologists, students, writers and investigators who still come, in increasing numbers, to examine them.

A foundation known as the A.R.E. (Association for Research and Enlightenment, Inc., P.O. Box 595, Virginia Beach, Virginia, 23451) was founded in 1932 to preserve these Readings. As an open-membership research society, it continues to index and catalogue the information, initiate investigation and experiments, and promote conferences, seminars and lectures. Until now, its published findings have been made available to its members through its own publishing facilities.

This is the first volume in a series of popular books dealing with those subjects from the Edgar Cayce Readings.

This volume presents data from 2500 Readings given by Edgar Cayce from 1925 through 1944, and deals with psychological problems rather than physical ailments. Such subjects as deep-seated fears, mental blocks, vocational talents, marriage difficulties, child training, etc., are examined in the light of what Edgar Cayce called the "karmic patterns" arising out of previous lives spent by an individual soul on this earth.

Karma, as he saw it, was a universal law of cause and effect which provides the soul with opportunities for physical, mental and spiritual growth. Each soul (called an "Entity" by Cayce), as it re-enters the earthplane as a human being, has subconscious access to the characteristics, mental capacities and skills it has accumulated in previous lives. However, the "Entity" must also combat the influence of lives in which such negative emotions as hate, fear, cruelty and greed delayed its progress.

Thus the "Entity's" task on earth is to make use of its successive rebirths to balance its positive and negative karmic patterns by subduing its selfish impulses and encouraging its creative urges. One of the most provocative concepts deals with the logical why and wherefore of apparently "needless" suffering.

The purpose of this volume is to present in simple, straightforward language some of the strange and exciting stories from the Edgar Cayce records which can help one to achieve a practical philosophy for every-day living.

—Hugh Lynn Cayce

10

CHAPTER ONE

"HAVE I LIVED BEFORE?"

On the warm afternoon of August 10, 1923, in a hotel room in Dayton, Ohio, the famous American seer Edgar Cayce woke from a self-imposed hypnotic sleep to receive one of the greatest shocks of his life.

As he listened to the stenographer read back a transcript of his words, Cayce, the most devout and orthodox of Protestants, a man who had read the Bible once for each of his forty-six years, learned with increasing bewilderment that he had stated flatly and emphatically that, far from being a half-baked myth, the law of reincarnation was a cold, hard fact.

His first fear was that his subsconscious faculties had suddenly been commandeered by the forces of evil, making him their unwitting tool; and he had always vowed that if ever his clairvoyant powers were to play him false, he would permit no further use of them.

Now, with his confusion mounting, he sat and listened to Arthur Lammers's excited account of what he had said. Lammers had requested these sessions. He had paid Edgar's expenses all the way from Selma, Alabama. And, though Edgar had been diagnosing and helping to cure the ailments of the sick with his "Physical Readings" for over twenty years, he had never been asked to expound on the forbidden territory of the occult before. Lammers, on the other hand, had made a thorough study of psychic phenomena and Eastern religions at a time when such pursuits were frequently confined to elderly ladies at phony seances trying to trace their pet pugs in a canine hereafter.

Lammers was as jubilant as Edgar was dismayed. The questions with which he had bombarded the sleeping psychic had all been categorically answered. The last of Lammers's doubts had been swept away.

And Edgar was at another—and perhaps the most critical—milestone of his uphill path through life. His first impulse was to turn and run. Merely to entertain the possibilities that a man lived more than one life as a human being on this planet seemed to him sacrilegious and contrary to all the teachings of Christ.

It was even a repulsive concept—illogical, defeatist, and macabre. The best of good Christians found it hard enough to keep firm their faith in Christ's promise to His believers that He went to prepare a place for them in His Father's house. But, sacrilege apart, the unfamiliar words that had emanated from his own mouth were almost gibberish to him.

Unlike Lammers, his education was confined to a literal acceptance of the Bible. He accepted it verbatim, had taught it verbatim in his Sunday Schools, and had drawn total spiritual comfort from it. Thus he was the least equipped clairvoyant Lammers could have chosen to voyage into such strange, uncharted waters.

What would have happened if Edgar had begged

to be excused and taken the next train back to Alabama? Perhaps a great deal more than we can rightly measure. Certainly greater issues would have gone by the board than the minor one that this book would not be in your hands. Certainly the psychiatrists would not have locked horns in controversy over *The Search for Bridey Murphy* in the mid-fifties —and inconclusive as that case may or may not be, it served as another milestone in Edgar's pilgrimage toward the eternal verities. Though he had been dead for eleven years, the attention attracted by Bridey publicized his philosophy in areas where it had never penetrated before, enabling his words to bring that much more aid and comfort to the sorely tried, the lonely, and the disenfranchised who had drifted from their own denominations, yet found no solace in the arid wastes of agnosticism.

It was only when Edgar conquered his doubts that day in Dayton and permitted Lammers to continue with his questions, that a new concept of reincarnation saw the light of day. This concept neither challenged nor impugned the teachings of Christ, but laid the foundations for a spiritual philosophy powerful enough to withstand the secular cynicism of this most turbulent of centuries.

Edgar Cayce made it a rule never to convert or convince by tub-thumping or "blinding with science." He left all judgment to the discretion of his hearer, and this book's only purpose is to give as clear a picture as possible of his theory of rebirth.

Over twenty-five hundred people went to him to learn of their previous life histories on this planet. The first logical question must be: "Did it do any of them any good?"

The answer is yes, in the cases where the "Readings" were seriously studied and their counsel applied.

It was to be expected that a fair percentage of lazy people, while prepared to recognize the home truths and timely warnings, still left their Readings to yellow on the shelf while they continued on their unrepentant ways. But the great majority were the gainers, to one degree or another. Some even transformed their lives from moral drudgery to purposeful use. Edgar taught that all human natures have one thing in common: they are only operating at full potential when their concerns are directed away from self-preoccupation and towards the assistance of their less fortunate brothers.

The most straightforward place to begin, then, must surely be with the study of two of these Life Readings in detail.

Once we have followed the practical application of previous experience to a man's present endeavor, we can more comfortably move to the broader implications of reincarnation. These will logically include the inflexible laws to which reincarnation conforms, its implied presence in orthodox religion, and the reasons why it has suffered such rejection at the hands of Western civilization.

On August 29, 1927, Alice Greenwood asked for a Life Reading for her younger brother David, who had turned fourteen three days earlier. Though Alice had already received her own Life Reading, her brother was personally unknown to Edgar Cayce. Edgar's wife, Gertrude, usually conducted these sessions, but on this occasion the only people present were Edgar's father, Leslie, substituting for Gertrude, Gladys Davis, the stenographer, and Beth Graves, a visitor.

Gladys Davis was Edgar's permanent secretary, a woman whose impeccable record of staunch and faithful service continues to this day.

All that was known of David Greenwood was that

14

he was a good student, bought his own clothes and schoolbooks by working as a newsboy, and liked to collect stamps. Beyond this, the sister possessed no special insight into his character.

It should also be made clear at this point that Edgar never undertook a reading except at the request of the subject or someone responsible for him. Once in self-induced hypnosis, he would answer to no other voice save that of the conductor of the questions. Any deviation from this procedure would result in silence, or his curt statement: "We are through for the present," whereupon he was given the suggestion to return to consciousness.

When this procedure was in any way violated, Edgar was in grave personal danger. On one occasion he remained in a catatonic state for three days, and twice had been given up for dead by the attendant doctors.

In response to Alice Greenwood's request, Edgar pursued his usual routine of reclining on a couch, hands folded across his chest, and breathing deeply. Then his eyelids fluttered—the signal for the conductor to close them and make contact with Edgar's subconscious by giving the suggestion for the Life Reading. In this case, Alice's written request for help for her brother was read. Unless this procedure was timed to synchronize with the fluttering of his eyelids, Edgar would proceed past his trance to a deep normal sleep from which there was no rousing him until he himself chose to awake.

CONDUCTOR: "You will have before you the Entity, David Roy Greenwood, born August 26, 1913, between Perry and Hale Counties, eight miles north of Greensboro, Alabama. You will give the relation of this Entity and the universal forces, giving the conditions which are as personalities, latent and exhibited, in the present life; also the former appearances in the earth's plane, giving the time, the place, and the name, and that which in each life built or retarded the development for the Entity, giving the abilities of the present Entity and that to which it may attain, and how."

A pause followed, during which Edgar's subconscious made contact with the subconscious of David Greenwood. (Had this reading been only concerned with the physical health of the subject, it would have been imperative that Edgar be told the exact geographical location of the boy at that moment, just as a tracking station must know the precise location of a satellite before it can make radar contact.) Then he began to speak in a quiet, unemotional undertone.

His first comment was that most of the boy's present characteristics consisted of latent instincts rather than recognizable traits responding to an effort of will. "We find indications, then, of one who is strong of body, yet with inclinations and tendencies towards physical defects which afflict the body by manifesting themselves in the digestion, or physical body. Hence the Entity should be warned against indulgences which may bring about strain and stress on the digestive system."

At this time there was no indication of any kind that the boy would eventually suffer from digestive trouble. It was an excellent example of Edgar's power of precognition. He then proceeded to laud the boy's friendly nature, but suggested he learn to curb his quick temper before it became a problem.

He warned that without responsible application of will power and a stable religious faith to guide him, the boy's impulses might continue to hamper his course of action throughout his life.

According to the unconscious memory the boy retained of his previous lives, his best chance for success was to associate with businessmen whose trade pertained "to materials, clothing, and of such nature. These will be the natural trend and bent of the Entity . . . for with the ability to make friends, the turn is seen towards nobleness of purpose . . . hence the training which the Entity needs under such conditions should begin, as soon as it may, to supply the correct groundwork for such a development."

He then proceeded to describe the boy's life immediately before this one.

It spanned the last years of Louis XIII and the early years of Louis XIV in France. Edgar referred to an approaching rebellion that could well have been the public uprisings against the Queen Mother and Cardinal Mazarin which lasted intermittently from August, 1648, until their final subjugation by the Prince of Conde in July, 1652. David's name then was Neil, and he occupied a substantial place at the King's Court, a kind of Master of the Robes and arbiter of fashion, personally responsible for the King's wardrobe.

Neil served his royal master faithfully, and Edgar made the point that he would stand to reap the benefits of his devotion to duty in this present life—a kind of good conduct medal, as it were, handed down from one self to the other.

What other characteristics did he inherit?

"There is seen, in the present, the urge to be particular with himself as to dress, and the ability to describe well the dress of a whole roomful of people, if he sets his mind to it."

It should be noted that the Reading occasionally employed cautious, sometimes pedantic phraseology, and for a very good reason. The subconscious mind of Edgar Cayce seemed to be dealing with the colloquial French of the seventeenth century, which it must then have transposed into the modern English idiom of his conscious mind.

The subconscious does not consist of tangible matter; only thought exists. Therefore, all languages are one. The danger of misinterpretation could only begin when Edgar spoke aloud. Thus his perpetual concern, once he had successfully transferred the "mental pictures" from his subconscious to the "teletype" of his conscious mind, was to retain the true original sense.

This care and caution became more and more evident as Edgar receded further and further back in time, and was confronted not only by obsolete idiom, but languages which made muscular demands on the throat and lip-muscles which his own would have been totally incapable of reproducing. Here his task was not so much to translate from one language to another, as to paraphrase unintelligible symbols into their nearest modern equivalent.

In short, he had to "crack the code," much as archeologists have had to reduce ancient sign languages to their approximate grammatical equivalents.

Edgar then proceeded to the life before the boy's French incarnation as Neil. This was on the isthmus of Thessaloniki on the Aegean coast of Greece. There, in a town called Solonika, he lived as a tradesman called Colval.

No exact date was given, but the times were referred to as unsettled, leaving one to assume that one form of government was being overthrown and replaced by another, enabling Colval to attain to a position of power which he subsequently misused. Therefore he forfeited some of the benefits he might otherwise have passed on to himself in the present. Nevertheless, "the influences in this life in the present are seen in his ability to fit himself into any place or position among whatever people he finds himself associated." He was also told, with truth: "Especially

18

is the love of family, and of those closely associated with same, seen from that experience."

The next serial life might well have coincided with Alexander's invasion and conquest of Persia.

Whatever invading power it was, it suceeded in dividing the country against itself. The boy's name was then Abiel and he took advantage of the times to rise to the status of court physician. Here the intrigue and corruption had its effect on him, but even though he again misused his authority, he was still commended for standing his ground when he faced the threat of persecution by his conquerors.

The influence on his present life was also seen in his innate desire "to study chemical compounds . . . the urge toward a desire to be a physician." This was perfectly correct; but instead of being told to encourage it, he was advised to put more store by the later experience as a tradesman in Greece.

In other words, the boy was warned away from his daydreams of becoming a great surgeon, the obvious implication being that he was not only economically and temperamentally unequipped for it, but also that his penchant for intrigue at the Persian court would restimulate facets of his nature that were better left dormant.

From here Edgar proceeded back to times so ancient as to border on prehistory—Egypt during one of its invasions by an alien race. It now became possible to identify the recurring factors in the path of this soul's progress. Both in France and Persia he enjoyed the privileges of royal favor. His familiarity with court procedure in Persia clearly enabled him to adapt his instinct, or flair, to his environment in France. Living twice in countries which had been overrun by invading cultures, the tumult and unrest had given him a clear insight into the psychology of crowds.

In Egypt his name was Isois, and once again he was able to make himself invaluable to his conquerors. From a humble beginning he rose to authority as a type of lay preacher who enjoyed the trust of the common people. As a result, the priests of the new dynasty used him as a go-between and "general interpreter" of the new form of worship.

"Hence he was among the first in the land to take on a special class of raiment, or garment, to distinguish self from other peoples."

The boy was told that his life had gained such luster from his concern for the welfare of the man in the street that relics still remain among the ruins of Egypt which commemorate his sanctity. After his death he was worshipped as a saint or minor god. "The Entity gained in that experience, and the gain manifests in the present, in his ability to apply himself to the masses as well as to the individual."

Egypt was invaded many times in its long history, but the presence of priests among the conquerors suggests that this period predated the Babylonian and Ethiopian invasions, and belongs as far back as the early Aryan invasions from the North.

This would place the time at about 10,000 B.C., which would seem far enough back for any soul. But next Edgar came up against the controversial subject of Atlantis, which science flatly dismisses as legend, and which Edgar Cayce defined as three huge bodies of land spanning what is now the Atlantic Ocean, possessing in common a civilization far in advance of our own and a practical command of nuclear energy which contributed to its own destruction and inundation. Large groups of survivors reached South and Central America and North Africa, and one group, not so easily assimilated because of its isolation, survived as the Basque race in the Pyrenees between France and Spain.

The material on Atlantis in the Cayce files is imposing enough to warrant a book of its own, and reference to it will of necessity occur in subsequent chapters of this one, but it is only necessary at the moment to establish the fact that its civilization spanned a period of two hundred thousand years, the last of its islands finally subsiding in 10,000 B.C.

"Before that, the Entity was in the Atlantean land when the floods came and destruction ruled the land, (and) was among those so destroyed. The The name then was Amiaie-Oulieb."

Most significantly, he was heir to the throne; so from his very beginnings, the blood of royalty was familiar to him. Despite his death by drowning, he had lived long enough to indicate that he lacked the discipline and dedication necessary to his station, but "the present (evidence of that incarnation) is seen in the ability to know materials, especially those that apply to wearing apparel."

Thus we find that in only one of his lives was he lacking an affinity for fine cloth and ceremonial vestments, even though the lives delineated by Edgar Cayce were not necessarily the only appearances the boy made on earth. (Indeed, his cycles suggest that he may well have been one of the members of a tenacious soul-group who pride themselves on the number of times they are reincarnated—almost as if some sort of Olympic Championship were involved! But these were the only lives that had a constructive bearing on his problems in the life on which he was now embarking. This became apparent in the final summing-up of David Greenwood's potential talents at the close of the Reading:

"As to the present abilities of the Entity, then, it is seen that many conditions arise which are to be met by the Entity in the application of himself to the environs of the present experience.

"First beware of those conditions which might bring detrimental forces to the physical well-being through the digestive system. Then, in this channel, follow specific diets and the correct application of food values for the physical well-being.

"In the mental and the body building, the Entity needs to apply himself first to that which will give the more perfect knowledge of his relation to Creative Energy, *i.e.* to the spiritual lessons which may be gained from a study of the Master's experience in the earth's plane as the son of man.

"In the material sense, apply self toward salesmanship and to the abilities of meeting the needs of man as pertaining to business relations.

"Keep self physically, mentally and spiritually fit, for in service the greatest blessings are given. Choose thou whom thou will serve; for no man can serve two masters.

"Keep the law, as is befitting to man's relation to God. Keep self unspotted from the world. Not as eyeservice, but as service of the heart to the Maker.

"We are through for the present."

The Reading was duly typed and forwarded to the boy's parents. It made so little sense to them that the boy was never given it to read. Fortunately, his sister was not so easily discouraged. She put the Reading in a safe place, and the case does not appear in the files again until seven years later, Aug st 22, 1934.

At this point the twenty-one-year-old David Greenwood was the main support of his mother and other sister. He was earning a modest salary as the circulation manager of a small-town newspaper, and had little or no promise of substantial advancement. His mood was both frustrated and restless when Alice finally presented him with his Reading and suggested he apply its counsel to his problems. His response was not much warmer than his parents' had been. There was nothing wrong with his digestion; he had no interest or aptitude for the clothing market; the idea of rebirth left him cold; and the possibility that he was some kind of repressed couturier was utterly ridiculous. However, he did admit that almost anything was preferable to spending the rest of his days in the obscure penury of the newspaper office.

Even so, it was not until the spring of 1940 that David's sister persuaded him to make use of an introduction she had obtained for him to the two partners of a third-generation clothing factory which confined itself exclusively to manufacturing uniforms. Alice had been aware that the partners were familiar with the work of Edgar Cayce and held it in high regard. Thus David's Life Reading left no doubt in their minds that he possessed a natural bent for their particular trade, and without further ado they offered him an opening as a traveling salesman. His main line was high school band uniforms, but he also catered to civic groups.

In the following year, David developed such a gift for anticipating his customers' needs that he added several southern states to his territory, outstripping every other salesman in the company, even though he was the youngest and least experienced.

In February, 1943, he was classified 4F by the Army. The reason: food allergies, the origins of which predated the Reading's warning that he could look for trouble with his digestive system!

Then gas rationing, crowded hotels and overburdened railroads wrote *finis* to his flourishing career as a salesman. So David volunteered to work in one of the largest Army induction centers, where an average of fifteen hundred officers a week were outfitted for combat.

By July of the same year he had been promoted to O.C.S. Clothing Shop. When the war ended, he returned to his old firm to be placed in sole charge of the retail section, while the two former owners concentrated on reorganizing the wholesale department as a separate corporation.

It is not surprising that the grateful Greenwood continued to work closely with Edgar Cayce, and a revealing fact emerged from the subsequent Readings: the weak digestion he inherited was a direct consequence of his love of rich food at the French court, where the gourmet Neil literally destroyed his body by his excesses in gluttony. (Gout was probably the least of the agonies that attended his death in that life.) The fact that Greenwood was confined to the most Spartan of diets in this life was not only restitution for the harm he did himself at the King's table; his own subconscious was also warning him never to inflict such needless and unattractive punishment on his physical self in any of the serial lives that still awaited him!

This is by no means a unique example of the 2,500 Life Readings made by Edgar Cayce, but it conveys in a clear-cut line of progression how the latent abilities of a fourteen-year-old boy, which would otherwise have remained fallow and unsuspected throughout his lifetime, were apparent to Edgar Cayce, correctly identified by him, traced to their source, and presented to the boy in terms of practical application.

Edgar lived long enough to see David Greenwood inherit his rightful destiny.

No less singular was Cayce's power of prophecy in a Reading he gave, six years before he died, for Grover Jansen.

When he applied for his Reading in 1939, Grover Jansen was in a more fortunate position than David Greenwood. He was a nineteen-year-old student who had doubts about his future. After two years in college, he could find no occupation to which he responded.

Edgar left him in no doubt as to his natural bent. In his previous life, during the War for Independence, he had worked as an agriculturist whose duty it was to estimate the amount of produce the Army could expect to obtain from a given terrain. Thus, there was little he did not know about the fertility or barrenness of any given area in which major battles were to be fought.

"The Entity, in the name of Elder Mosse, was associated with Andre as well as with Arnold, Lee and Washington, in those lands about the upper portion of what is now New York State . . . hence we will find in the present that mountains and streams, the outdoors, all those activities which relate to physical prowess, have an innate, subtle influence upon the Entity in its choice of its dealings with others."

In the life before that, the youth had lived in the Roman Empire during its period of great expansion.

"There we find the Entity was among those who were the choice of at least three emperors—the early Caesars, but not the first—for activities in England, Ireland, portions of France, portions of Spain and Portugal, as well as the northern coasts of Africa and Grecian lands and the Palestine land. All of those were a part of the Entity's activity.

"For the Entity was among those (and there was only one other) who had the ability to judge as to what could be best produced in the varied lands with the least effort to supply the greater benefit to the empire in its various spheres of activity.

"Hence we find that every activity of nature comes under the Entity's judgment—whether to furnish adornment, food, a means of exchange, including the feathered tribes or those that were the fur bearing, or the production of seeds or woods of various kinds.

"In the present, then, as indicated, the Entity has the ability—from that very sojourn—to become a judge of those influences for conservation . . . the name then was Agrilda.

"Before that we find that the Entity was in the land now known as the Egyptian, during those periods of reconstruction following the inundation of the Atlantean land, of which the Entity had been a part.

"For the Entity, though younger than some of those who were in authority, soon grew in favor in that Egyptian land, not only for instructing and edifying the various groups, but aiding the bond of union and strength that comes from united efforts for the better conservation . . . the name then was Ex-en.

"As to the choice of how the Entity will act in the present then: as to whether it will fulfill that purpose for which it entered, or glorify self or a cause, or an individual, that must be decided by the Entity alone.

"In those fields of conservation—whether it be of fishes in waters, birds of certain caliber, needs for food, or protection of certain portions of the land or timbers, or the better conservation of soil for certain seeds or crops—all these are the channels in which the Entity may find contentment and harmony.

"Of course, the land continues to grow—for it is God's footstool—but man's abuse of same can cause it to become no longer productive. But if there is the conservation of its strength—the lands, the timbers, and God's creatures that manifest through same—it is a continuous thing. For 'Ye grow in grace and in knowledge and in understanding' is applicable to man's secular life just as much as to his mental or spiritual."

Q: "Should I continue at Penn State College next year?

Cayce: "If there is a course in which this particular study is stressed, yes. If it is found that there can be a greater study through the Government's activity in those fields, choose that! And it will be opened if ye look for it!"

The youth followed the advice in his Reading promptly and to the letter. And just as Edgar had told him, he developed a natural affinity for wild life and conservation.

It was a thoroughly contented and fulfilled man in the National Park Service of the Department of the Interior who wrote to Hugh Lynn Cayce seven years later:

"Dear Folks: We are finally located for the summer at the south gate of this beautiful and biggest of our National Parks. It is a big thrill to me to have the title of 'Ranger,' since I have always looked upon these guardians of our natural resources as 'real men' ever since I was a little shaver. I'm starting in as 'Ranger-Naturalist' July first, which is an even bigger event in the climb up the ladder.

"Well, the bragging is over now, but I just had to

let you all know that the Readings have made me and my little family very, very happy since we at least know that we are on the right road.

"This Ranger-Naturalist job is a perfect opportunity to show the people a little of God's work untouched. Every stream is pure and good to drink, chock full of trout ready for fly. All of the old mountain men, as well as the Crow, Sioux and other Indian tribes, once roamed this very country so rich in history. The antelope, buffalo and elk and moose are as common as they were when the pioneers first cut a trail through this great wilderness. The grizzlies and black bear make one aware that some danger lurks behind each tree. . . . I find a spice here that I have never experienced before.

"Intend to return to the Agricultural College in September to finish up a few credits for a sheepskin, and then into the National Park Service for good maybe.

"Come on out—I'll give you all a complimentary pass!"

Then in 1951, he wrote from the Fish and Wildlife Service to a friend who was sufficiently concerned for her son's future to ask his advice: "If only Edgar Cayce were living now I am sure that a Reading would be the answer to many of those knotty problems that you are now dealing with. I was very fortunate in contacting the Association at an early age, and as the result of a Life Reading and several Check Readings, I have found the kind of work for which I am best suited.

"As you can see from the letterhead, I am no longer with the U.S. National Park Service. Last August we moved to North—— where I have assumed the title of U.S. Game Management Agent and enforce the Federal fish and game regulations in this State.

The Life Reading advised Government work in the conservation of natural resources, and I can assure you that I enjoy the position immensely!"

THE BOY WHO REMEMBERED

It would hardly be logical if the soul-history Edgar Cayce traced for himself were not both imposing and unique. But by the same token it is so complex and recondite that only a volume wholly devoted to its evolution could make it comprehensible to the orthodox layman.

Without trying to inflate him to a Grand Panjandrum, his spiritual antecedents place him in a high echelon of human souls. His various lives took him from sublime heights to plateaus in which he was neither particularly exalted, nor gifted with more than the normal five senses.

For example, in the life he spent on the American continent immediately prior to his return as Edgar Cayce, he had not been a minor saint. He had been a mercenary in the British Army prior to the War for Independence—a jovial rolling stone with an eye for the ladies and the bottle.

He was born in 1742 of swashbuckling Cornish stock—a Celtic race which in those days felt little if any love for England and gloried in smuggling and ship wrecking. He was christened John Bainbridge. Originally, he landed in America in Chesapeake Bay (significantly near to Virginia Beach which, like a Lorelei, had called him back to its shore in this life). His involvement in the intermittent skirmishes with hostile Indian tribes took him as far north as Canada, and finally confined his theater of war to Fort Dearborn, the site of present-day Chicago. The frontier life there was rough and rowdy, a foretaste of the shenanigans that were to paint the California boom towns scarlet in the following century, and he was a man of his own times in every sense of the word.

When the beleaguered Fort Dearborn finally fell to the Indians, he aided a large group of men, women and children to escape down the Ohio River on a clumsily assembled raft. They had insufficient supplies to sustain them and were unable to go a-shore to forage, the Indians having pursued them along both banks of the Ohio. One by one the unfortunates died of exposure and starvation, but Bainbridge's own life ended in an act of heroism; he died enabling a young woman to escape to safety.

Apart from this, his soul had made no great spiritual progress in that life, and it would merit no further comment, save for two singular links with his present life. The woman whose life he saved sought his help again in this life, and through her he was able to aid many of the souls he had known in Fort Dearborn, for as a group, they had remained intact, bringing their unfinished problems with them to be resolved in the environs of the Chesapeake peninsula. (See Chapter XVI.)

A minor but much more disarming fragment of evidence was forthcoming when the Cayce family first moved to Virginia Beach in September 1925. Edgar had accompanied his son Hugh Lynn to a barber's shop where the barber's son, a sleepy five-year-old, was fretfully awaiting his mother's return to put him to bed. His father had given him a box of animal crackers to keep him pacified, and when his drowsy gaze suddenly focused on Edgar, he trotted over to him and handed him the box. "Here," he said impulsively. "You can have the rest. You must still be awfully hungry!"

"Leave the gentleman alone! You know better
30

than to pester folks you don't know!" his father chided him.

"But I do know him!" protested the child, gazing up at Edgar with complete confidence. "He was on the raft, too! And you were real hungry then, weren't you, mister?"

"Thank you, young man," said Edgar gratefully. "I'll take just the one cookie," and then added in a confidential whisper, "and you're right! I was real hungry on that raft!"

CHAPTER TWO

IF WE HAVE LIVED BEFORE,
WHY DON'T WE REMEMBER?

The subconscious mind does remember its past experiences, but there is every good reason why the conscious mind is spared that rather dubious privilege.

Imagine yourself to be a soul before it returns to earth. Imagine yourself a diver seated on the deck of a salvage ship in the Caribbean. It is a calm, bright day. The water is smooth and transparent, the skies unclouded; only a slight breeze stirs.

Somewhere below you is the wreck of an old galleon, reputed to have been laden with golden bullion when it sank. You can even detect the shadowy skeleton of its few remaining timbers, though most of it is buried in silt. What you cannot see from the deck of the ship are the intricate cross-currents flowing at that depth; they are too far down to disturb the surface calm of the sea.

Because of the length of time you must spend submerged, you now don an old-fashioned canvas diving suit with lead-weighted boots, and a copper helmet is screwed into place over your head. Its small oval windows confine your vision. As you climb overboard, your body feels as if it weighs a ton. The sweet drowsy ozone you were breathing undergoes a deglamorization as it is pumped into your helmet through the airhose. As soon as you disappear below the surface, however, you adjust to weightlessness and sink down comfortably to the sea bed. It is all clear-cut and straightforward: your success is a foregone conclusion. You will merely have to reach the ocean floor to walk straight to the wreck, locate the treasure, dig it up, and then signal to be drawn back to the surface.

The only thing you have failed to take into account is the fickleness of the sea itself. As your feet touch the seabed, you find yourself fighting against a strong current. You pitch your full weight against it and start approaching the wreck. But the force of the current, pushing you first this way and then that, doubles the dead-weight of the cumbersome suit and helmet you are wearing.

Let us call this suit the physical body which the soul inhabits while it is on earth. All goes well with it while the currents are just right, and the light is just right, and you are in full control of it. But the filtering light may suddenly be obscured by clouds over the sun, and the ocean floor suddenly becomes grey and murky. The perpetual resistance of the crosscurrents begins to weary you; your muscles begin to ache. What had promised to be such a simple and rewarding task from the safety of the deck of the ship now becomes complex, confusing and frustrating. Nothing is made any easier by the appearance of a couple of hungry-looking twelve-foot sharks, who skulk menacingly nearby. As you reach the wreck, your lifeline and airhose tangle with the upturned beams of the wreck. You struggle afresh to disentangle them. The air coming down the hose is impeded. You begin to feel short of breath. You also begin to wonder what on earth you are doing down there, and whether any amount of treasure will be worth the discomfort. You try to remember the chart you had studied so carefully on deck, which clearly indicated which part of the wreck would contain the treasure. Now you are no longer sure which is the stern of the wreck. You begin to experience what Thoreau describes as "quiet desperation." Time tends to stand still. You feel you had been on the sea bed in your unwieldy diver's suit since the beginning of time, and that you will remain there for all eternity. The normal life on shipboard becomes more and more an unreal dream—something that you yourself had never experienced personally. The voices filtering down to you through the speaking-tube become equally inhuman and unreal. The *only* reality is the battle you are waging not to be pushed this way and that by the currents. You are keeping such an alert eye on the slowly circling sharks, who seem to be imperceptibly moving closer and closer, that you have little time to search for your bearings and concentrate on your original mission.

At last such weariness, claustrophobia and defeat overwhelm you that you can barely signal to the men above to haul you back aboard. On your way up you develop a case of the bends, and when you are finally dragged aboard and rescued from your stifling suit, you are more dead than alive.

In the period it takes you to recover, while you lie on your back gulping in the fresh air, the memory of those interminable hours down below, in their turn, became the vague dream. The unreality now is the period you spent on the ocean floor; the reality is now the deck of the ship and the security you feel in the companions around you.

The whole memory-process has been reversed.

In like manner does the human soul re-enter the world of the living too often too over confident, and likewise it returns after death to its original state with too little confidence, having forgotten that the two separate worlds coexist, and that one is just as real as the other.

"ONE MAN IN HIS TIME PLAYS MANY PARTS"

If you prefer a more tangible frame of reference to account for your apparent lack of karmic memory, think of yourself as a professional actor.

Put yourself in the shoes of the great Shakespearean actor, Sir Laurence Olivier, whose theatrical genius has given us definitive portrayals of Henry V, Hamlet, Richard III and Othello. Each one of these roles is a perfect and fully resolved creation in its own right; none of them derivative of the others. Olivier actually had to live these roles to imbue them with such intensity and conviction.

Between each of these achievements, Olivier, the professional actor, has had time to rest and take stock of his progress toward the position he now enjoys. He may be the greatest living classical actor in America and Europe, but away from his profession, his problems are no different from yours. He makes appointments with his dentist, has income-tax headaches, colds in the head and an occasional hole in his sock. But the difference becomes instantly apparent when he stands in the wings of the Old Vic Theater, about to make his first entrance as Othello.

Is he worrying about Laurence Olivier's tax problems? Most certainly not. Laurence Olivier is fast becoming a vague dreamy blur in his memory. His sole identification is with Othello. He concentrates only on the emotions he must soon evoke. The canvas scenery disappears, and a real street in Venice takes its place. The voices of the other actors continue, but are now emanating from the throats of flesh-and-blood sixteenth-century Venetians.

To a very real extent, Olivier is in self-induced hypnosis as he makes his entrance onto the stage.

Now—imagine him passionately declaiming, drawing on the last reserves of his emotional energy, yet maintaining split-second discipline as he times each syllable—and tell me if he would have time to dwell proudly on his press notices for his Hamlet, or glow with nostalgia at the memory of the ovations he received for his Richard III, or suddenly wish he had used a different accent and makeup in his film of Henry V.

Let me assure you he would be incapable of remembering anything beyond Othello's immediate infatuation for Desdemona. Even during the intermissions and offstage waits, he would still be Othello —an Othello relaxing, perhaps; as the body does in sleep; but still Othello. Not until the final curtain has fallen and the audience left the theater, not until his costume and makeup are removed, can he be in any sort of condition to discuss the critical pros and cons of his previous triumphs as Henry V, Hamlet and Richard III.

And, if you take the parallel further, not all Olivier's theatrical portraits were successful. But it would be needless sabotage of his own confidence, if he never permitted himself to forget that he once allowed himself to .be hoaxed into making an abysmally dilettantish film version of *The Beggar's Opera*. What kind of performance could his "Othello" audience expect of him, if his mind were so obsessed by that one failure that it impelled him to stop short in the middle of his performance as Othello to whisper to Desdemona: "Ye Gods, old dear, what an absolute jackass I made of myself as MacHeath! I've no right to be out here taking their money!"

What would happen to the rapport he had so carefully built up between his Othello and the audience?

Apply this to yourself. Suppose you were allowed voluntary access to all your previous lives, and one day, by chance, you stumbled across the memory of having been the greatest monster in history!

How would you deal with the horror, the belated remorse? How would you deal with the fear that your soul might be in such arrears that you would have to put in another million lives of bitter compensation to atone for the harm you did your fellow-souls in that one incarnation? What hope would be left you?

Actually this situation can never arise, for the simple reason that it would throw the whole karmic law of cause and effect out of balance, and the workings of that law are fixed and unalterable. No soul will ever be permitted such calamitous knowledge of its own past blunders. Whatever the debt a soul owes to its fellow-souls, it will never be called upon to settle it until the soul has progressed to a sufficiently mature level to make such compensation possible and practical. Meanwhile, from this point on, let us jettison the idiotic concept that "karma" is brutal and senseless punishment unleashing itself on us unworthy sinners.

"For the Lord does not tempt any soul beyond that which it is able to bear," said Edgar Cayce. But many times he had to exorcise the dark tenets of Predestination and Original Sin from the hopelessness and confusion in the minds of the people who came to him for help.

"Most individuals in the present misinterpret karmic conditions," he said. "Each soul or Entity should gain the proper concept of destiny. Destiny is within; it is of faith; it is as the gift of the Creative Forces. Karmic influence, in this case, is rebellious influence against destiny."

"The Entity puts a stress upon karma," he reproached one of his questioners. "If ye live by law, you must judge by law; but if ye live by faith, ye judge by faith.

"This is not intended as criticism, nor as sarcasm," he told another, "but that ye may know that it is the law of the Lord that is perfect—not men's conception of it. The law will be fulfilled. Will ye do it, or let someone else do it? . . . He who seeks will find. He who knocks, to him it will be opened. These are irrefutable, these are unchangeable laws."

And here he analyzes it in greater detail:

"Karma is a reaction which may be compared to the reaction within the body when a piece of food is taken into the system. The food is translated into a part of the body itself, penetrating to every cell, and influencing the health of the body and mind.

"Thus it is with a soul, when it enters the body for an experience in the earth. The person's thoughts, along with the actions which result from these thoughts, are the food upon which the soul feeds.

"These thoughts and actions, in turn, have been generated by thoughts and actions behind them; and so on back to the birth of the soul.

"When a soul enters a new body, a door is opened, leading to an opportunity for building the soul's destiny. Everything which has been previously built, both good and bad, is contained in that opportunity. There is always a way of redemption, but there is no way to dodge responsibilities which the soul has itself undertaken.

"Thus a life is a way of developing, a preparation for the cleansing of the soul, though it may be a hard path, at times, for the physical consciousness and the physical body.

"Changes come, and some people say luck has intervened. But it is not luck. It is the result of what the soul has done about its opportunity for redemption."

And here, in the simplest of terms, he presents the Law of Grace which supersedes atonement: "Karma is rather the lack of living up to that which ye know ye should do. As ye would be forgiven, so forgive in others. That is the manner to meet karma."

Throughout the Readings one comes across cases of individuals whose karmic sin was their determination to clutch onto their obsolete guilt and shame, rather than make a positive effort to balance them by the "forgiveness of others."

Obviously no one can be forced, either by his God or his fellow man, to forgive himself, or anyone else, until he himself decides to. He is at liberty to remain in his chosen purgatory for as long as he prefers it to any other state.

But until he has evolved himself to a sufficiently enlightened outlook to pull himself up by his own bootstraps, what will he gain by asking: "Why don't I remember?" Isn't it more circumspect to say: "I'm glad I don't remember!"—even if this means he is denied the gratification of reviewing those lives in which he was a ministering angel to his fellow souls and died loved, honored and respected?

All the good achieved in any life remains permanently with the soul. A soul can never undo the good it has done, and later in this book we can examine how this can be set against the law of cause and effect by the application of the Law of Grace.

CHAPTER THREE

MAN'S SUBCONSCIOUS IS IMMORTAL

In the early days, the difference between the "waking" and the "sleeping" Edgar Cayce was as fundamental as the difference between East and West Berlin. There was, of course, no antagonism between the two minds, either, even though one was vulnerable and human, and the other was spiritually insulated against the "sea of sorrows" to which man falls heir.

Perhaps the simplest frame of reference is the ship-to-shore radio—you cannot talk on it and listen at the same time. It is simply a mechanical device which enables the man at sea to make contact with the man ashore. As for itself, it records no impressions and retains no memory of the words that enter and emanate from it.

Toward the end of Edgar Cayce's life, there was definite evidence of a merging of the two levels of consciousness, but in his early years, he was as startled as the next man to learn he had given medical counsel to an Italian, in fluent and flawless Italian. Nor was the complicated medical terminology that rolled off his tongue any more intelligible to him in his waking state than was the fluent Italian.

Perhaps the most popular misconception foisted on him was that he was a kind of secular Moses crying in a metaphysical wilderness. What *did* give his mind uniqueness was its apparent ability to recall its own beginning in Creation.

His purpose—perhaps his whole purpose, for all we know as yet—was to serve as a "paver of the way" to those who believe their heritage began in God. "What I can do today, every man will be able to do tomorrow," is a recurring theme in his philosophy.

That every soul possesses the same potential is implicit in the words he uses to describe the soul's first appearance on this earth.

"In the beginning, when the first of the elements were set in motion that brought about the sphere called 'earth plane,' when the morning stars sang together and the whispering winds brought the news of the coming of man from his indwelling in the spirit of the Creator to manifest as a living soul, this Entity came into being with this multitude."

If we bear in mind that at this time the orthodox "waking" Cayce's interpretation of the Bible was diametrically opposed to his "sleeping" interpretation, it is interesting to compare the above statement with this passage from Job 38: "Then the Lord answered Job out of the whirlwind, and said. . . . 'Where wast thou when I laid the foundations of the earth . . . when the morning stars sang together, and all the sons of God shouted for joy?' "

Even as they were awaiting creation, according to Edgar Cayce, some souls were already predestined to use their new-found free will to serve God's purpose on the earth, while others were equally designated to use their free will to do as they chose. . . . The newly-born earth offered them an opportunity

42

to usurp God's role as Creator and become petty Creators in their own right. In short, the souls brought sin with them. It was not here awaiting them "in the flesh" on a planet where even animal evolution had not yet begun. Indeed, the density of "solid" matter, as we know it now, lay millions of years ahead. Thought was the original motivating force. Dense matter was a subsequent mutation of thought after it "bogged down." To simplify—thought can be compared to molten lava—malleable, perpetually moving, changing, capable of resuming any form. Solid matter is its inanimate aftermath, responsive only to the chisel and the hammer.

Hence you will find throughout the Readings the perpetual reiteration that "Thought is the Builder" —the wet clay responsive to the potter's hands—and that the survival of the soul depends utterly on its power to mold its destiny at the subconscious level, where the clay is moist enough to respond.

Just as a series of chain reactions alters the atom from a harmless particle of solid matter to the mushroom cloud that obliterated Hiroshima, the chain reactions of positive thought can eventually release the soul from solid matter and return it to the freedom of its fluid state at the astral level.

It is because we lack the equivalents of such convenient scientific terms as "atomic fissure," that we are reduced to referring to the process which releases the soul as "the tragedy of death."

This is akin to throwing away the potato and glorifying the potato peel.

It is far simpler to think of the soul in terms of Telstar. It takes two booster-rockets to free it of gravity and set it in astral orbit. As soon as the rockets fulfill their function, they burn out and fall away, just as the flesh body—the earthly shell of the soul—burns out and falls away in death, to be followed by the expended "ego," the discarded conscious mind of the earth shell.

The soul is no longer entrapped in matter. It is free. All that it retains from its sojourn in its earth shell is the total recall of its worldly experiences, now safely stored in its "memory bank." But only the "conscious" mind has been discarded.

The subconscious mind has survived because it neither consists of, nor depends on, matter. It now becomes the conscious mind of the soul, and will continue to function as such until the soul returns into the earth's dense matter to begin its next life.

Meanwhile the superconscious mind assumes the functions relinquished by the subconscious mind, and the soul is now articulate as it could never be on earth. The "ecstasy" that certain Saints achieve is probably akin to a momentary recapturing of the exhilaration the soul enjoys at this level of existence.

When the time comes for the soul to return to earth and assume its next body, the process is quite simply reversed. The conscious mind returns to the subconscious level, and the subconscious mind returns to the superconscious level, where it subsides back into a womb-like sanctuary in the flesh body. It neither seeks nor desires emotional association with the pursuits of the subconscious mind and the new-born conscious mind, as they accustom themselves to their new ego.

Only very rarely, in a very few cases, can the superconscious mind be contacted—and then only by expert deep hypnosis. (While Edgar Cayce was able to contact his superconscious by means of his own quite unique form of self-hypnosis, it must be born in mind by the reader that he is the exception, not the rule, at this present level of our universal development. He is a glimpse of ourselves as we will be tomorrow.)

The "new-born" conscious mind, then, can never be older in age than the new body which is temporarily housing it. The new-born's accumulated store of wisdom, its caution and its intuitive appraisal of both itself and its fellow men all lie at the subconscious level. Thus the only friend and counsellor to which it can turn is its own subconscious mind. Moreover, it can only make this contact while asleep in the "dream state," or by the enlightened process of meditation. Here, by dint of self-discipline, it trains itself to sit and listen for the "still small voice of conscience."

In its waking hours, at the conscious level, the new-born must meet again all the novel distractions of material existence, picking its way as best it can across the stepping stones that span the treacherous crosscurrents of life, avoiding—if it heeds its "still small voice"!—the excesses of self-indulgence that have so often tripped it and sent it headlong into the waters churning round it.

Has it any means of anticipating in advance the problems it will have to face?

Yes, indeed, if we liken the lives of the soul to the installments of a serialized novel in a magazine. As your soul dies at the end of a life, "to be continued in our next issue," is parenthetically added in small print to that installment. When you appear again in a new body, you do not start from scratch; you pick up exactly where you left off.

If you had failed to curb a passion for pitching rocks through greenhouse windows in the life before, you can resign yourself to being born into the equivalent of a greenhouse, where you will have to learn to enjoy the discomfort of being at the "receiving end" of the rocks. If you grin and bear it while the panes are bashed out one by one until the score is evened, you will not be doing so badly. But it you collapse in self-pity, insisting that you have done nothing to deserve your fate, you are obviously in a sad way, and your overall gains are doomed to be minimal.

Edgar Cayce himself had no false pride about admitting that some of his lives could have been better spent—that he had often given in to anger and impatience—that the fleshpots of prehistoric Egypt, for example, had offered sufficient temptation to distract him from the thorny path of total advancement.

It was as much to put his own spiritual house in order as to help his fellow creatures that he shouldered the onerous responsibility of his clairvoyance in this life.

Where did he obtain his information, when he set out to give a Life Reading?

In a talk he gave at the Cayce Hospital in 1931 he explained it in these words: "Let me tell you now of an experience of my own. I feel that it was a very real experience, and as near an illustration of what happens at death as it would be possible to put into words. On going into the unconscious state, on one occasion, to obtain information for an individual, I recognized that I was leaving my body.

"There was just a direct, straight, and narrow line in front of me, like a shaft of white light. On either side was fog and smoke, and many shadowy figures who seemed to be crying to me for help, and begging me to come aside to the plane they occupied.

"As I followed along the shaft of light, the way began to clear. The figures on either side grew more distinct; they took on clearer form. But there was a continual beckoning back, or the attempt to sidetrack me and bring me aside from my purpose. Yet with the narrow way in front of me, I kept going straight ahead. After a while I passed to where the figures were merely shadows attempting to urge me on, rather than to stop me. As they took on more form, they seemed to be occupied with their own activities.

"Finally I came to a hill, where there was a mount and a temple. I entered this temple and found in it a very large room, very much like a library. Here were the books of people's lives, for each person's activities were a matter of actual record, it seemed. And I merely had to pull down the record of the individual for whom I was seeking information. I have to say as Paul did, 'Whether I was in the spirit or out of the spirit, I cannot tell'; but that was an actual experience."

FREE WILL IS STRONGER THAN DESTINY

When he touched on the previous lives of the people who came to him for help, Edgar Cayce constantly insisted that karma was memory, thus the laws of cause and effect were elastic. The soul, like a "trusty" in a penitentiary, can always get its sentence "reduced for good behavior" by cooperating with authority. One lifetime of genuine sacrifice to the welfare of others, such as Schweitzer's or Father Damien's, might well equalize five or six sterile existences where progress stood still and the soul fell behind in the parade.

Free will, in short, is always stronger than pre-ordained destiny. No soul is ever so encumbered with old debts that it must drearily resign itself to pay and pay and pay.

But we must also allow for the fact that the soul can sometimes advance itself by methods that need not be immediately apparent to our powers of conscious reason. The blind man healed by Christ, for example, was not blind because he had sinned, but because his soul was gaining stature from the experience of blindness.

It is absolutely essential to understand and accept this simple concept before proceeding to deal with the more complex issues which will arise, as we treat individual cases in more detail.

However sore the straits may be in which you find yourself, you put yourself there by your own previous indifference to the laws. Whatever laws you broke, you broke of your own free will, the free will given you in the beginning by your Maker. You alone chose to be where you are at this moment. This, at least, allows you the dignity and self-respect of knowing that you made your own mistakes—even if it destroys the convenient sugar-coated alibi that you are the victim of an angry, vengeful and palpably half-witted Jehovah, who controls you with invisible strings from the flies of a most naively ill-conceived marionette-master's Hereafter.

To conceive of a fretful God of Vengeance at the controls of this immaculately operating Solar System is to credit a tin lizzie full of Mack Sennett cops with the ability to break up traffic jams on a crowded eight-lane freeway.

That is why the hell-fire doctrines of original sin and the enlightened tenets of true religion have never been able to coincide.

The only God the sleeping Edgar Cayce knew was a loving God of infinite mercy, who has already forgiven us all.

As the reader begins to take more heed of the processes involved in the theory of reincarnation, let him bear in mind that every one of its laws stem from such a concept, and could not function otherwise.

CHAPTER FOUR

PHYSICAL AND EMOTIONAL KARMA

THE WAGES OF VIRTUE, AND THE WAGES OF SIN

When Paul Durbin was thirty-four years of age, with a wife and a child to support, he was stricken with multiple sclerosis, or creeping paralysis, and his right leg and arm began to wither.

Though Paul's family was all but destitute, good friends rallied to his aid. They paid for his hospitalization, obtained his Physical Reading, and even administered the massages which the Reading advised. His condition soon began to improve.

But significantly, the Reading also made reference to a past incarnation in which he had indulged his negative passions to excess.

"The Entity is at war with itself. All hate, all malice, all that will make men afraid, must be eliminated from the mind. For, as given of old, each soul shall give an account of every idle word spoken. It shall pay every whit. Yet the Entity knows, or should know, that there is an advocate with the Father.

"For, as given, 'Though ye wander far, if ye call

I will answer speedily!' Then, right about face! Know that the Lord liveth and would do thee good, if ye but trust wholly in Him!"

In short, a soul had but to acknowledge by its penitence that it had gone astray, and help would be forthcoming in exact proportion to his sincerity.

The warning fell on deaf ears. Durbin, saturated with bitterness and self-pity, dismissed such an idea as rubbish and demanded to know why Cayce had failed to cure him miraculously and instantaneously. He even vented his frustration on the people trying to help him, playing them off against each other until they regretted their involvement.

Nevertheless his condition improved for a while. When the improvement failed to stabilize, he complained even more bitterly than before.

His next Reading was phrased in blunter language: "This is a karmic condition, and there must be measures taken for the body to change the attitudes towards conditions, things, and its fellow man.

"First there should be a change of heart, a change of mind, of purpose, a change of intent. If this is done, then keep up the massages and the use of the appliances suggested. But all the mechanical appliances that ye muster will not aid complete recovery, unless thy soul has been baptized with the Holy Spirit! In Him, then, is thy hope. Will ye reject it? The body is indeed the temple of the living God, but what does it appear to be in the present?

"Broken in purpose, broken in ability to reproduce itself.

"What is lacking? That which is life itself, that influence or force ye call God. Will ye accept, will ye reject? It is up to thee!

"As long as there are hate, malice, injustice—those things which are at variance to patience, long suffering, brotherly love—there cannot be a healing of this body. What would the body be healed for? That it might gratify its own physical desires and appetites? That it might add to its own selfishness?

"Then, if so, it had better remain as it is!

"We are through—unless ye make amends."

This Reading was deliberately selected for its uncharacteristic austerity. The correspondence in the A.R.E. files is mute testimony to the recalcitrance of this patient, determined not to stir a finger in his own behalf, demanding the restoration of his health as his due.

Why did Paul Durbin suffer? Why do any of us suffer, if it comes to that?

"All illness is sin," said Cayce, and he does not necessarily mean sin committed consciously in the present life, but sin expressing itself as illness because it has not yet been expiated by the soul.

Karma, the abacus on which the gains and losses of the soul are scored from life to life, is often wrongly and unjustly confused with retribution. It is too meticulous and dispassionate for that; its ultimate purpose too benign. But while it is acting as a painful cure for an even more painful relapse, it can be bitter gall indeed.

Apparently a certain type of mortal suffering can be a salutary astringent to the torpors of the subconscious mind, when all subtler warnings have failed to persuade the ego to exert itself in its own best interests. "Whom the lord loveth, he chastizeth," has more kindness than irony in it, when viewed in this light.

The Readings divide karma into two rough categories—emotional karma and physical karma. Each of these has, of necessity, its positive and negative aspects—its good and bad.

Under the negative emotional heading, we find

such symptoms as incompatible marriage, alcoholism, impotence, neuroses such as manic depression and paranoia, mental perversions, and even possession in its medieval sense.

On the physical side, it manifests itself in such defects as deafness, blindness, speech impediments, and the killer diseases such as leukemia and multiple sclerosis.

Through his entire life as a seer, Edgar Cayce devoted the bulk of his efforts to the successful diagnosis of bodily ailments. On many occasions, however, he traced them not to physical causes, but to an inevitable moment of truth at the subconscious level, when self must answer to self. The murderer who shed innocent blood in one life will balance the scale in another by symbolically shedding his own. More than one case of leukemia was directly attributed to this reckoning.

But the remedy need not always be so drastic as it was in the case of Paul Durbin. The Law of Grace is a perpetually available alternative to the soul—the working off of accumulated debts, by unselfish dedication to the welfare of others even less fortunate than itself—in Edgar's own words, "what you sow you reap, unless you have passed from the carnal, or karmic, law to the Law of Grace." Most souls seem to hover between the two extremes.

The next case of physical karma deals with a woman who successfully overcame the challenge which faced her.

Stella Kirby, a quiet, retiring woman, divorced and with a child to support, was advised by a friend to take up nursing. She had no sooner completed her training than she was sent to apply for a private post at nearly twice the normal fee. She was interviewed by the housekeeper of an imposing mansion, a pleasant woman who took an instinctive liking to her and hired her on the spot. The house was well staffed and elegantly run, the food was excellent and her quarters almost luxurious. All this, coupled with the generous salary, was more than Stella had dared hope for. But when she was taken to her patient's bedroom, she was confronted by a man of fifty-seven in a state of imbecility. His bed was encased by an iron cage, and in it he sat systematically shredding every article of his clothing, blank-eyed and incapable of all normal functions. He could neither speak nor respond to speech. He had to be fed like an infant, sometimes forcibly, and he resisted all and every effort to keep him clean.

Dismayed, but determined to do her best despite the revulsion she felt, Stella entered the cage to give him his bath, and the moment she touched him she was overcome by such nausea that she had to retire to the bathroom and vomit.

When the revulsion showed no signs of abating, she realized she had to give up the job and the security she badly needed. Fortunately, she was able to journey to Virginia Beach and appeal personally to Edgar Cayce for help—and thus, one of the most bizarre of his case histories unfolded.

Twice before, the paths of Stella and her patient had crossed. In Egypt he had been her son. The revulsion she felt for him stemmed from a life in the Middle East when he had been a wealthy philanthropist of high standing, greatly honored for his generosity. Privately, however, he retained a kind of seraglio of young women who were obliged to participate in his abnormal sexual practices, and she had been one of the unfortunate women involved.

The memory of the degradation and disgust had returned the moment she had touched his flesh, while he, poor devil, again surrounded by every material luxury and comfort, had met his karma—with a vengeance. It is hard to conceive of a soul more destitute and debased.

Yet Cayce insisted (as he did in every similar case) that the crippled mind was capable of responding to love—that Stella must, in short, learn to love him if she ever hoped to surmount her own karmic barriers. To leave the house would be no solution: the bond between them would simply continue, unresolved, into their future lives.

Years later, Stella described her first reactions to her Reading. The idea of reincarnation was completely new to her, yet she instinctively responded to it. God had never been clear or real to her before; now she found herself able to comprehend Him. All her life she had felt such a compassion for cripples that before the birth of her daughter, her one fear had been that the child would be born with deformed legs. This stemmed from a life she had spent in Palestine, where she had nursed and healed the weak and maimed—an experience which could now reward her a hundredfold. Even the housekeeper who had employed her had been with her in Palestine, and this had accounted for the mutual liking they felt for one another as soon as they met.

Stella remained, but the idea of conveying love to the pitiful creature she was nursing all but defeated her. Several times she felt she must admit defeat, but the Readings always urged her to keep trying, and eventually her patient began to show signs of responding. He obeyed her utterly, ate his food instead of rejecting it, began to keep himself clean, and no longer tore his clothes to shreds. And as she moved about the room, his eyes followed her with dog-like devotion.

Her love had conveyed itself to his paralyzed brain, as Cayce had insisted it would; and with the

realization that he was once more loved, he was released from his own immediate hell. He might well
have lingered on for an interminable span of years,
yet he was able to die peacefully within two years,
and Stella was able to go forward into a balanced
and rewarding life of her own.

The Readings were too compassionate to refer to
the relationship between the two when she had been
his mother in Egypt, but since there is no effect
without cause, she would hardly have been subject
to his obscene fetishes in the Near East unless she
already owed him a debt. One can assume that she
had failed her son in Egypt, either by neglect or
rejection, at a point in their mutual destiny where
her help could have prevented him from plunging
off onto the self-annihilating path which brought
them together again in the Middle East. Here again,
where her love might have wakened a response in his
profligate soul, she withheld it, thus stretching out
the misery to span yet another life.

THE CASE OF THE MONGOLOID CHILD

Physical and emotional karma combine again in
the following case history of a man and his wife who
had been closely associated in at least two of their
previous lives. Both could be called highly developed
souls, but they were nevertheless meeting a challenge,
a test, which they might well have failed without the
help of their Life Reading.

The six-year-old child of Myra and David Cobler
was a Mongoloid. The Coblers asked if their conduct
in their past lives was to blame, and the answer was
phrased with great delicacy.

Not all the lives "were pretty," and though the
present life had been so far disappointing, Myra's

sublimated longing to be a novelist could yet express itself if it would use for material the very lessons she was learning from the sorrow in her own home. Her passionate nature, her longing for affection and her deep spiritual loneliness could all be turned to positive account. In regard to the love and patient care the child needed, as she gave of it with more and more freedom, so could she build a life of beauty for the next child she would bear.

"Do not blame self," Edgar told her, "do not blame thy companion. Do not blame God." She and her husband had reached that plateau where "self must meet self" and jointly put their records to rights. If they succeeded in this, they would so aid the soul of their child to free itself from its own karma that it would never again need to incarnate in a deformed shape.

The child's soul, said Edgar, "is thy problem with God, not to be put aside until He, who is the Giver of Life, sees fit to call it home to prepare for the better life that ye have made possible in thy kindness to thy fellow man."

What had Myra done to reach such a fate? Her previous life had been wretchedly spent in a frontier post in the early middle west under the name of Jane Richter; yet for all its squalor it had laid the foundation for her intense longing to make her home secure and congenial in this life.

Her Reading then traced her back to Palestine "when the Master walked in the earth." The name of Dorcas established her as a woman of Greek or Roman origin, as did her sophisticated skepticism of the miraculous powers attributed to the Messiah. Not having bothered to seek Him out and judge for herself, "the Entity made fun of, yea rebuked those" who believed he was indeed the Son of God. It was not until the day of Pentecost that His path crossed

56

hers. When she saw the outpouring of the Holy Spirit, she was converted, but felt it was too late to atone for her apostasy. "But it is never too late to mend thy ways," Edgar exhorted her. "For life is eternal, and ye are what ye are today because of what you have been. For ye are the co-creator with thy Maker, that ye may one day be present with all of those who love His coming."

In this Palestinian life, her husband's fate-line converged with hers. He was one of the Seventy chosen to spread the gospel throughout the land. He failed because he took certain of the Teachings literally instead of symbolically. Particularly had he been offended by the purely spiritual content of "Except ye eat of My body, ye have no part of Me."

His name was Elias and he was a friend of two of the disciples, though he "leaned more towards the staid Andrew than the boisterous Peter," for he could reason with Andrew whereas he could only argue with Peter.

The Reading then suggested that if both David and Myra reattuned their memories to the arguments they had once heard from these two disciples, it would awaken positive attitudes in their own thinking in the present.

"For the law of the Lord is perfect. It converteth the soul if it is used, not abused, in the application," the Reading continued. "As the Entity learned in his experience as Elias, healing of the physical without the change in the mental and spiritual aspects, brings little real help to the individual in the end."

One last sojourn is suggested—and only very lightly—in the Egypt of 10,000 B.C. where David, under the name of Atel El, had served as an aide to the surgeons in a Temple of Healing, and Myra had been educated in the cultural arts in a similar type of Temple.

This period saw the development of a sub-race of primitive souls from a retarded evolution, only slightly above the animal level, to the full stature of bodies "fashioned in God's image." These humanoids or mutants feature extensively in the Atlantean records as a primitive form of antediluvian life, the last faint echoes of which linger in Shakespeare's Caliban and in the fauns, centaurs and minotaurs of Greek mythology. They were for the most part defenseless and pitiful beasts of burden which had been used for slave labor by the Atlanteans, and the purpose of the Temple was to hasten their evolution by corrective surgery. This involved the use of the laser, followed by ritual purification in the name of the One God. In these far distant beginnings, then, we may infer that these two souls were first taught to care for the maimed and helpless; and that the troubled soul who came to them in the present as a mongoloid child did so because it remembered their aid and compassion when it was first struggling to acquire human status.

This would account for the compassion and deep concern the Reading conveys to all three of them throughout. If they have strayed off their appointed path, one feels they have strayed very slightly. The bonds forged in Palestine were too strong to fail them entirely.

Which one of them had gone most recently astray? David, perhaps.

His last life before his present incarnation had been as William Cowper, "a keeper of the records" at the time of the American Revolution when Washington was rallying his demoralized forces at Trenton, prior to turning the tide of battle towards eventual victory. Here William Cowper, in charge of the victualing of that section of the Army, was involved in some kind of disaster which resulted in loss of limb to some of the volunteer patriots.

"Here a word of warning would be given," says the Reading cryptically. "Beware of a body that is malformed, or where some portion of a limb or activity is amiss; it may bring thee great distress."

Cowper had apparently been one of a group that stumbled into a British ambush. In his anger at the carnage, Cowper held his own officers responsible, even though it was not the fault of "those in authority, but was by accident." The shock of seeing his companions killed and mutilated had burned deep into his memory, however. Unable to forgive his officers in that life, the inability to forgive had manifested itself in his present life as a major hindrance to his peace of mind. The sight of a cripple would automatically rekindle his old bitterness and sense of injustice, thus inflaming and clouding his judgment—even when it affected his helpless child.

His urgent need was to practice forgiveness, tolerance and understanding in all his dealings with others. Only thus could he approach his emotional problems constructively.

The almost paternal kindness in which these two Readings were couched leave little doubt that Myra and David Cobler cared for their Mongoloid child until "He who is the Giver of Life saw fit to call it home."

This might be an example, then, of the Law of Grace superceding the law of karma, thus sponging the slate clean of accumulated debts.

What of the child itself? An indication is reflected in another Reading for a chronically retarded child. This soul held a position of authority in the court during an English incarnation, much akin to the voluptuary Lord Buckingham, whose rapacious exploitation of his privileges and influence contributed to the beheading of Charles I and even had repercussions in the French court, where his liaison with the Queen all but destroyed her.

"The Entity turned away from those who were without hope, who were disturbed in body and mind, preferring to indulge the appetites in self. Here we find the Entity is overtaken, and what he has sown, he is reaping."

To the parents who faithfully nursed the child with protective affection, the Reading was particularly approving. "For through your love and service, the soul-consciousness of this Entity may become aware of the power of true, abiding love to inspire individuals to protect those who are dependent on their care, for the soul of this Entity is entering an awakening in the present. Sow the seeds of truth, hope and mercy, of kindness and patience, that this soul shall learn at last that 'I am my brother's keeper!' "

Irene McGinley first came to Edgar Cayce's attention when she applied for a Physical Reading at the age of seventeen. An attractive, intelligent and talented young girl, she was already bedridden with an erosion of the femur, and her doctors had recommended amputation of the leg at the hip to prevent further spread of the cancer. She was a member of a large well-to-do family, and the wife of an elder brother also lived in the house. Though she had children of her own, Kit, the sister-in-law, was very ably filling the role of Irene's companion and part-time nurse. The treatment suggested by Irene's Physical Reading obviated the need for the amputation and placed her on the road to recovery. But we are concerned here with the Life Reading she subsequently requested.

Yet again we find physical and emotional karma meeting at a predestined crossroad. All the people involved were aware of mutual ties, but on the surface there were none of the character conflicts that appear so often in situations of this kind. All that manifested itself was the apparent injustice of Irene's affliction.

"One refined of taste," the first Life Reading described Irene. "The mental abilities are keen; love's influence bringing the greater experiences . . . as in the seeking for something in a constant manner in the developing of mental and physical abilities in self."

Straightaway the tone is optimistic. It presupposes a normal and productive life. Cayce calls her a dreamer, a builder of castles in the air, and suggests that writing is the form of creative expression best suited to her, but that it should always be anchored to reality. In the life before, she had been an early settler in America. Pretty speeches meant little to her, for she judged people by their actions, not their good intentions. She was honest and forthright in her religious convictions, and skilled in sewing, knitting and spinning.

But the life before that found her in the Rome of the Emperor Nero during the persecution of the Christians, the daughter of a wealthy and influential government official. Among the women of the household she observed with discreet caution the impact of Christianity on their lives. Here we find the first clue to her misfortune—"laughing at another's sincerity has brought physical defects . . . as does the holding of grudges, as does selfish interests."

Cayce began the second Life Reading with a deft analysis of the soul's memory bank. This, as it registers its experiences in the Akashic Record, "is to the mental world as the cinema is to the physical world."

Now we find that Kit, her present sister-in-law,

had been the daughter of one of the guards assigned to the Roman household. There was presumably a close bond between the two girls, for they shared a deep love of music, and Kit was treated as an equal. Kit was also a secret convert to Christianity, and Irene found herself being drawn more and more to the teachings of the Master, although she took care to conceal her sympathies when she attended the persecutions in the Coliseum. This was perfectly logical and understandable conduct when one took Nero's insanity into account. Any high-born Roman lady expressing leanings towards Christianity stood a good chance of joining the martyrs in the arena.

Cayce's allusions to unhappy love affairs are always tactfully phrased, but we are led to assume that Kit attracted the affection of a man Irene herself favored. In Irene's angry desire to punish the man she betrayed her friend to the authorities so that her lover could witness his loved-one's death in the arena. Seated beside him in the audience, she laughed at his horror as the girl he loved was mauled to death by a wild beast before his eyes. Irene's laughter had obviously stemmed from a hysteria of jealousy, and not from callous glee, but the karmic bond was forged. Retribution followed swiftly. The man, broken-hearted, never recovered from the horror of the spectacle, and she was forced to watch him waste away before her eyes. Her conscience was further tormented whenever she heard the music Kit and she had sung and played together, "especially of the lyre, harp, or of the zither." Then her remorse caused her interminable suffering.

"Hence in meeting same in the present, the Entity passes under the rod, as it were. She is now being pitied, laughed at, scorned for the inability to take part in any activity that requires the full use of the physical body.

"The Entity may now overcome those things that have beset, knowing how life is to be met: no scorn, no sneer, but with patience and fortitude, with praise, with the giving of pleasure in music, in kindnesses, in gentle words, in bespeaking of that which may build for a perfect mind, a perfect soul, a perfect body . . . for the weaknesses of the flesh are the scars of the soul, and these can be healed only by making the will one with His, being washed, as it were, in the blood of the Lamb."

The punishment here seems to be not for the laughter itself, but for the *crime passionel*—the cold betrayal of a rival whose religious faith she secretly shared.

What of Kit's own karma?

In prehistoric Egypt and again in Arabia, she had gained and lost. In Egypt she developed the talent for nursing which enabled her to care for Irene in the present; but she had been vain and jealous of her social position in Arabia, and resentful when age caused her to relinquish it.

In the Roman period she had made a great spiritual advance: the sermons of Paul himself, delivered at the secret meetings in the catacombs, had converted her so thoroughly that she died bearing Irene no grudge.

In the next life, however, as a child of twelve in a French inn, she witnessed the recognition and arrest of Louis XVI and Marie Antoinette just as they were about to escape to safety on the eve of the Terror. The fever-heat of the times stimulated an ambition in her to be part of the Revolution, and as soon as she was old enough she sped to Paris, where the turbulence of the times soon lifted her to a position of influence in political circles, and where her self-aggrandizement eventually brought about her own downfall.

In her present life, she had restrained this ambition in herself and pursued the wise course of marrying and concerning herself with her family's well-being. The help and care generously given her younger sister-in-law did much to balance the karmic debts she had acquired elsewhere. She even overcame her inborn fear of animals, derived from her death in the arena.

Irene, in her own turn, restored to health by her Physical Reading, followed Edgar's advice to take up the harp, and discovered she possessed an inborn talent for it to a professional degree. Retired from the concert stage, she still uses the harp even today, in the kindergarten she conducts, to create and mold a love of music in her charges.

Thus Irene and Kit represent an example of the positive application of both emotional and physical karma. Indeed, it is seldom one comes across the manifestations of one without the other operating somewhere in accord nearby.

A notable exception is the following case, where emotional karma came into its own with none of the overtones of physical disability—only a soul inheriting the rewards awaiting it for "good conduct."

Two years before Edgar Cayce died, Norah Connor, a widow of thirty-one, applied to him for vocational guidance. "Yes," began the Reading, "we have the records here. What a muddle-puddle; and yet what a talented soul!

"Here we find an Entity who may be said to combine all that is beautiful, gracious and lovely; and all the mischief-making that one might imagine.

"Suffering has cleansed the mind much. It has set it towards helping others. This is marvelous, for it is well for most individuals even to be in the presence of this Entity.

"What a wonderful companion this Entity would

64

make for a school that would teach spirituality as well as graciousness in the home, in motherhood, in things having to do with the making of a home! These should be the activities of the Entity.

"True, through the periods of the present conditions (World War II), give thyself to the activities in Red Cross Service. For ye can encourage many in such a way that they will never again grumble at their hardships.

"But when these conditions have passed, begin and work with groups in music or art, in social science, even in political economy, any undertaking that deals with the emotions, with all forms of character-building for teen-aged girls. Do apply yourself in these directions, for abilities here are far, far beyond the ordinary.

"Do not allow the ravings of others to deter thee from what ye know to be thy spiritual and mental duty. Do keep that beauty of love, of hope, of gentleness, of graciousness, that is the innate characteristic of the Entity."

The Reading then proceeds to delineate her previous life as the wife of a frontiersman in the early settling of America. There she learned to tend to the women and children, hold the settlement together, provide against the harassment of the Indians by setting up storehouses for food, and dressing the wounds of the men after the raids. "Then in the name Anna Corphon, the Entity created the environs of home life in surroundings that would have put many a strong-hearted man to shame. For, despite the hardships and those conditions that existed among the natives, the Entity builded friendships, having learned that the self should not offend and not be offended by others. With such an attitude one will, indeed, eventually find peace in self. There

65

must be harmony in self before ye can bring it to others.

"The Entity has found it, loses it at times; but keeping thy trust in Him, will never weary in well-doing.

"Before that, the Entity was in the Palestine land when the Master walked in the earth. The Entity was among the children at Bethsaida who were blessed by Him. Thus the desire, ever active and latent since that experience, to emulate His laughter, His thoughtfulness, His care for others. For as the Entity applied herself through that period when there were trials, then in the name Samantha, she encouraged those who became weary and weak from the temptations of the flesh which arise at times in every human in materiality. Hence the Entity is a most gracious hostess, a most loving individual with those close and those apart."

One of the written questions she put to Edgar Cayce was: "Is there any indication of what church I should join and associate myself with?"

"Remember, rather, the church is within self," he answered. "As to the denomination, choose one, whatever its name, not as a convenience for thee but where ye may serve the better. Let it be thy life proclaiming Jesus, the Christ."

"Any other advice?" was the final question.

"Why tell beauty to be beautiful? Just keep sweet," she was told with unwonted gallantry.

A fairly clear portrait emerges from her letter of gratitude to Edgar Cayce: "The Reading certainly expresses my most inmost desires and aspirations. My dominant desire and interest has always been in homemaking, and I love serving people. I find that at the present time I am very much interested in social studies—geography, history—and English as related to present day community and world affairs.

"As to the music and art referred to, my interest has been more in its use in connection with worship services. I think that the course in college that I liked best of all, and in which I received an A, was Fine Arts in Religion.

"I know I must have 'peace and harmony' in myself if I am to give it to others. And when I lose that peace and harmony I'm like a lost soul struggling to get back on the right path again.

"I have changed jobs so many times that it seems as if I should stick to one over a year. I realize that I can only decide on opportunities as they come along, but I do get in such a stew. (As you say 'What a muddle-puddle!')"

For the rest of the war years Norah devoted herself to the Red Cross and discovered she had a natural propensity for organization. She rose to a position of executive responsibility equaled by very few. Emergencies brought out the best in her, and at the end of the war she was decorated for her services. She continued to serve with the Red Cross, specializing in rescue work in disaster areas.

As Hugh Lynn Cayce notes in his check report, made in 1957, "Mrs. Connor continued to work for the Red Cross, as was suggested in the Reading. We wondered whether the rescue work along the Delaware River and Louisiana took her into the areas associated in her Reading with the 'pioneer days when she overcame insurmountable difficulties and did a good job.'

"She also described her problems with a superior official in the disaster work, when the word 'ravings,' indicated in her Life Reading, might well apply to the supervisor's criticism of her over-zealousness in giving help and comfort to the flood survivors.

"She is now employed in Boston University in charge of a dormitory of 150 girls. She intends to take courses that will prepare her for work in a smaller establishment where she can devote herself to the education of younger girls, as suggested by her Reading. She also indicated that she enjoyed Girl Scout work, especially the outdoor life, camping, etc.

"As a matter of interest, the interview with her was most pleasant throughout, and in my observation, confirmed the Reading's assessment of her character in full measure."

FEAR OF CHILDBIRTH

"I'm almost on the eve of insanity and suicide, the most miserable woman on earth and almost a dope fiend," reads an excerpt from one of the more extensively documented cases. Flora Lingstrand, born 1879, was forty-six years of age when she wrote for help. Her troubles began with a neurotic mother whose terror of death in childbirth increased with each successful birth of her six children. Flora's childhood was warped by her mother's lugubrious harping on her one fixation. And when Flora eventually embarked on her own marriage, she found her reason paralyzed by the inherited phobia. Her husband was a decent and sympathetic man who did all he could to understand and help, but birth control was apparently out of the question, and she was so obsessively terrified of pregnancy that eventually she separated from him. He still helped her with what money he could afford, and in an ill-advised moment she decided to have her ovaries removed.

In her incoherent letters to Edgar Cayce, Flora implied that radium was used, and that the "bromides" they subsequently administered, created in her an addiction to narcotics. This was compounded by chronic over-eating and haphazard consultations with various psychiatrists.

"I cannot go to another sanitarium, for the analysts do not talk anything but sex life . . . they say my suppressions have caused my nerves and dread of children, and after they told me the trouble, it stuck in my mind until I cannot bear my husband near me. I am afraid all the time, and fear is horrible," Flora wrote.

Flora was a tragic figure. Her self absorbtion blinded her to the needs of others, and in that area lay her only chance of salvation. To this day, her voluminous letters make pathetic reading, yet one cannot quite reject the impression that her occasional bursts of remorse for the suffering she is causing her husband are "words for the sake of words."

Her Life Reading patiently assures her that her case is not as hopeless as she is determined to make it, but states quite clearly on its first page that the source of the trouble lies in the need for the soul to correct and overcome its old preoccupations with self-aggrandizement, "desires of the flesh," and lack of consideration for the human rights of others.

"One lovable in many ways, one with high aspirations, many never attained! The goal is always whisked away just as she is about to attain it. In the purpose, good. In the actions from within, and of the use of will towards self, not good. Its relations with others, in the greater portion excellent . . . with itself, negligible."

Her previous life was as Sara Golden, one of the steelers who came to Roanoke in Carolina—the "Lost Colony" which disappeared without trace in 1590.

Here she was forced to witness all her children "taken and scourged in the fire, and the Entity lived in dread throughout her remaining days." As her reason failed her, she began to curse God in fury for allowing her children to be destroyed. "This, in the present, brings the dread of the Entity for the bearing of children . . . and has brought destructive forces into the Entity's (present) sojourn."

She had, in brief, returned without hope of forgiveness from the God she had reviled. But this is a manifestation of her own guilt, not the retaliation of a secular deity; therefore her sin is only against self.

The life before that was squandered at the French court of one of the Charleses, which means prior to 1515 . . . "a somber age of traitors and cut-throats." As one of the King's clerks given to excesses of debauchery, the forfeiting of subsequent domestic happiness had its beginnings. We have to search all the way back to ancient Greece to find the soul as yet uncorrupted. And in prehistoric Egypt she had "stood immaculate and tall" as a priestess in one of the Temples of Initiation.

The Reading ends with no promise of quick panaceas: "The Entity may gain only through service to others, for in serving self without respect for the good that may come into the lives of others, self blocks the way. When we build a barrier between ourselves and our associates, our friends, or our families, this we must, of our own volition, tear down, would we fill that place that is necessary for each and every individual to fill, that has its existence in the physical plane.

". . . . Those spirit forces which are innate may become so subjugated by the desires of the flesh that they become as nil. Yet these are ever ready to be awakened and to exercise their prerogative in the life of each and every individual. But self must be subjugated before such may come about."

Following this is a suggestion that Flora develop

a latent talent for writing, and that she choose for her subject matter a positive philosophy that would have an uplifting influence on its readers.

Flora Lingstrand seized the help Edgar offered, with the frenzy of someone drowning, but one cannot but feel that despite the protestations of gratitude that poured from her, she had been expecting some kind of miraculous intercession which would exempt her from having to make any personal effort in her own behalf.

One will often come across this tendency to expect of Edgar, contrary to his explicit warning, that he be not a counsellor but an extension of the Angel Who Troubled the Waters at the Pool of Bethesda. The act of immersion alone was expected to constitute a complete cure. Whereas Edgar never deviated from his one principle: only faith in a benevolent God enables the soul to reassess itself and put itself to rights.

By the same token, Cayce was never a man to mince words if he was confronted by lassitude or self-pity trying to pass itself off as a hapless casualty of karma.

"Is there some karmic debt to be worked off with either or both of my parents?" a young woman asked him. "And should I stay with them until I have made them feel more kindly towards me?"

"What is karmic debt?" he answered crisply. "You have made this a bugaboo! It is not a karmic debt between you and your parents; it is a karmic debt to self which may be worked out between you and your associates in the present! And this is true for every soul!"

"Would it be best to remain in the same apartment with my family for the present, or try to borrow money enough to get a place of my own?"

"It would be better to remain," he advised. "If the

antagonism between self and family continues, then change. Separation at the moment would leave not only animosity and a feeling of spitefulness on the part of self, but also on the part of the family, which would build that which you have learned, or been taught, to call karma."

Her next question was suitably chastened:

"What is there wrong about my personality which is holding me back, physically and mentally?"

"Nothing," he said amiably, "save improper evaluation of self in the present experience!"

ARROGANCE AND SELF-RIGHTEOUSNESS

We now concern ourselves with the emotional karma of a beautiful girl in her early thirties, a compulsive drinker, who was involving herself in one promiscuous affair after another. When she was sober she bitterly condemned herself, but remained incorrigible. Her Reading informed her that her avid nymphomania originated in a French incarnation when she was a king's daughter. It was a period of immorality and materialism, and she had not hesitated to sit in judgment over weaker women than herself, leaving little room for tolerance or pity in her self-righteous condemnations. She ultimately retired to a convent to avoid further "contamination" by her fellow-creatures, obviously leaving a trail of persecution behind her.

"Ye condemned those whose activities were in direct disobedience to the law," her Reading informed her. "But he who is weak in the flesh, is his error the greater? For one should know that the condemning of others is already a condemning of self. Which is the greater sin?"

Hate and self-centered arrogance had also dogged

a woman who took her own life in a Persian incarnation. She had been the proud daughter of a wealthy tribal chief who was captured by Bedouins and given in marriage to a young captain who had fallen desperately and sincerely in love with her. This could have been an opportunity for soul growth, but to a woman of her ferocious pride it was intolerable degradation. When she bore him a daughter, she found no consolation in motherhood. Unable to overcome her hatred and contempt for her abductors, she committed suicide, abandoning her baby to its own fate.

Today, lonely and unmarried, she longs for a baby girl with such intensity that she is even prepared to adopt one. She is thwarted in this because she has been embroiled in an obsessive love affair which has dragged on interminably and frittered her life away. Of her incompatible lover, she asked: "Why have I only received unfairness from him, when I have tried so hard to be fair?"

"As he is treating you in the present, so you treated him in that Persian experience," Cayce told her. "As ye mete it unto others, it shall be meted unto you!"

The same boomerang struck a young man who had been a caricaturist in the French court of Louis XVI. He had lampooned those unfortunate members of the court who were unable to conceal their homosexuality. In this life he is mortified to find himself struggling against the same compulsion, and though his Reading was able to help him, it again pointed out that "Whatsoever we mete unto others, we mete unto ourselves."

The philosophy of the Life Readings takes on such a universality in the following excerpt that one is tempted to call it a definitive credo for every living soul, regardless of sex or age.

"From Saturn we find the sudden changes that have been and are a characteristic of the Entity—in this, Mars plays a part. When these two planets are together, there is an adverse influence, a wrath or madness, bringing great disturbance to the mental being of the Entity.

"Hence it behooves the Entity to keep before itself an ideal, not merely for the sake of being idealistic, but as a standard by which it can judge its own deeds. For the ideal of what is right can never apply only to self.

"For if ye would have life, ye must give it! As the laws apply in the spiritual, so do they apply in practice. For Mind is the Builder.

"If ye would have love, ye must show thyself lovable. If ye would have friends, ye must show thyself friendly. If ye would have peace and harmony, forget self and make for harmony and peace in thy associations.

"For each soul is in the process of developing itself to become fully aware of its Maker. And as thy Lord hath given: 'In the manner ye do it unto the least of these ye meet, day by day, so ye do it unto thy God.'

"Be not deceived and do not misunderstand. God is not mocked. For what man soweth, man reapeth, and he constantly meets himself!

"If ye attempt to meet it alone, by thyself, then it becomes karma. But do good, as He gave, to those that spitefully use thee, and then ye overcome in thyself whatever ye may have done to thy fellow man!"

"SUFFER LITTLE CHILDREN TO COME UNTO ME"

Perhaps the most moving case of emotional karma in its most positive sense belongs to Edgar and Gertrude Cayce themselves.

Their second son, Milton Porter Cayce, had been born on March 28, 1910, at 8:30 p.m. and had died two months later, May 17, at 11:15. Edgar, who had been able to save the lives of so many children, had been unable to save his own child, and though he never discussed the subject, the tragedy had haunted him until he dreamed, during the First World War, that he met and talked with a group of his Sunday School pupils who had been killed in the battlefields of Flanders. Still dreaming, he reasoned that if he had been allowed to see these young soldiers still alive and happy, there should be some way of being able to see his own son. At once he found himself in the presence of tiers of babies, and in one of the higher tiers he saw his own baby smiling down at him in recognition. He awoke consoled and never again grieved for the welfare and security of the child's soul.

Then, nearly twenty years later, on May 25, 1936, he began to give a routine reading on a thirteen-year-old boy, the son of a doctor, born in Peking, China, on March 31st, 1923. He began as usual by counting back over the years from the present to the date of the boy's birth, noting the vast change in his outlook in 1932 when his family returned with him to the States.

Then unexpectedly he announced that "those associated in this undertaking" were in a position to study the case at firsthand. "For this Entity, now called David Hoffman, entered the earth's plane in the previous experience for only a few weeks—on March 28, 1910, 8:30 in the evening, departing on May 17 at 11:15.

"The mother would know, in the present," he added, referring to Gertrude, and implying that she would respond in instinctive recognition once she saw him again. He explained that the boy had died because "there was too great a disturbance in the mind and experience, during that period of gestation, for the soul to remain." By the same token, there was little or no opportunity for the soul to develop. But now that David was established as having once been their son, "the knowledge and association of same will bring helpful experiences in the development of the soul of the Entity."

He then dealt in great detail with the potential physical weaknesses the boy faced. The digestive system was delicate, might adversely affect the colon and appendix . . . "be warned of these, that there be not a cutting short of the opportunities for the Entity; for . . . those weaknesses exist as a material overlap from other experiences in the earth."

In the life before his brief sojourn as Milton Porter Cayce, he had served as a secretary to Adams and Hamilton in Boston, during the framing of the Constitution; hence in the present he would find himself able to serve men in high authority without awe or confusion, "for the ideals of the Entity naturally are high."

In the life before that "the Entity was among the children of one Bartellius, in Palestine, and was blessed by the Master, Jesus. The boy was among those who later suffered material hardships for the causes held, not only by his people and his parents but for those tenets held by himself."

It was from this experience that he had developed his high ideals, for in every Reading where a child had once received the touch of Christ's hand in blessing, the memory remained indelibly in the soul-memory as a benediction.

His earliest life had been in prehistoric Egypt, one of the refugees from the subsiding continent of Atlantis. "The name then was Aart Elth. This, to be sure, was the Egyptian name for a consecrated teacher in the service of the Temple.

"Though young in years when journeying into Egypt, the Entity aided in the development of mechanical appliances for the cutting of stone in the temples of service, as well as the temples of sacrifice.

"Hence, in the present, these things (though of a much higher order) make for peculiar experiences at times, as does music, upon the whole of the bodily forces.

"These should aid the Entity in first learning to know itself, its own weaknesses physically, its own abilities mentally . . . and thus, in a coordinated, consecrated effort may great experiences come to the Entity in this sojourn . . . for, as the body-mind develops, each of these branches should be offered as an opportunity or outlet: those of a mechanical nature, those of a musical, or those of a biological nature, which would include insect life and its influence on man's environ."

When Edgar returned to consciousness, his wife told him with tears of joy that he had been aiding his lost son to prepare for his new life.

A year later, Dr. Hoffman brought the boy to New York to meet Gertrude and Edgar. David, of course, was never told of the link between them; but just as Edgar had warned her, Gertrude was so magnetically drawn to the boy that she had difficulty in concealing her true feelings.

It is hard to conceive of a more unique situation in the history of Edgar Cayce's tireless service of his fellow men. It served the double purpose of consoling the parents of a child they had lost, and aiding the parents of a thirteen-year-old boy to preserve him against the illnesses most likely to beset him in his formative years.

CHAPTER FIVE

THE ELEMENT OF FEAR IN EMOTIONAL
KARMA

THE ROOT CELLAR

Patricia Farrier, a spinster of forty-five, was told in her Reading that in her previous life she had lived and died near Fredericksburg, Virginia, under the name of Geraldine Fairfax, while America was still a British Colony. She was told that records, "even in stone," still existed. So she and her sister Emily journeyed to Fredericksburg in the hope of tracing them.

During their search, the sisters had occasion to put up at a small rural hotel one night. Having retired to bed healthy but tired, they soon fell asleep—a sleep from which Emily was awakened by a choking noise from her sister's bed. She turned on the light and found Patricia literally suffocating to death. Her face was red, and she was fighting desperately for breath, yet Emily was unable to wake her from the deep coma in to which she had fallen.

In panic, Emily sought help from the proprietor, but nothing would rouse Patricia from her coma, and she seemed to be on the verge of death. On the arrival of the doctor, she was brought back to consciousness with difficulty and normal breathing was finally restored. The two sisters fled the hotel that morning and hastened back to Edgar Cayce. In her subsequent Reading, Patricia asked: "Why have I so much fear in the present?"

She was told that she had been subject to many fears, in the physical sense, in her previous lives, and these had come through with her into the present as subconscious memories.

As a thirteen-year-old girl in Fredericksburg, she had been playing at "gardening" in the root cellar, where all the seedlings, cuttings, potatoes and herbs were stored on shelves during the winter. It was presumably a place where the child was forbidden to go unattended, and on that day a minor earth tremor shook the countryside, causing the floor of the farmhouse to cave in. The shelves collapsed and buried her under an avalanche of roots, bulbs and damp soil. She had smothered to death in such an hysteria of panic that it manifested itself in this life as claustrophobia, a terror of crowds, a fear of smothering. Its direct association did not manifest itself, however, until she and her sister had stayed the night at the hotel. This hotel must either have been built over the site of the old frontier homestead, or was sufficiently near to it for her memory to reenact the actual death throes of the child in the previous life.

Her Reading advised her to harness the energy she was expending in fear to a positive ideal of some kind, whereby she could profit rather than lose from its influence. Her karma offered her full reason to develop her capacity for deep religious faith. In Palestine at the time of Christ she had been a member of the household which witnessed the resurrection of Lazarus by the Master, and the New Testament was accordingly familiar to her at a high subconscious level of personal identification.

She took this advice and achieved success in full measure, developing a prayer group which devoted certain hours of its day to prayers for Edgar Cayce when his own energies were occupied helping others.

The immense dignity of Edgar Cayce's simplicity is movingly illustrated in the letter of gratitude he sent her:

"My dear Miss Farrier: It would be very hard indeed for me to express to you my appreciation of yours of the fifteenth. I realize a great deal more than I'll ever be able to tell you, how much your prayer group—as a group, and as individuals—have helped me. I have come to depend upon them a great deal. I feel very much as Moses must have felt when it was necessary that Joshua and Aaron hold up his hands! I am willing, but the flesh is weak—and it's very necessary that we have those upon whom we can rely when our own strength fails. I assure you I have found a great deal of strength in the efforts and the cooperation of every member of the group.

Thanking you, and with all sincerity, I am,
Ever the same,
Edgar Cayce   Dec. 18, 1931."

Patricia Farrier died of cancer in January 1939, and he corresponded with her to the end, advising her sister by Physical Readings how best to nurse her. When she asked how much longer she would have to "remain in this suffering condition," he consoled her with the assurance that it was in no way a punishment, merely the soul's completion of its lesson in patience, "even as Jesus in the Garden learned obedience through suffering."

Equally moving is the understanding Cayce showed

81

for Jane Clephan, a college girl of twenty-one with an almost disabling inferiority complex.

He commented at once on her inborn musical ability and urged its development. He also assured her that she had a latent talent as a concert pianist and teacher, once she developed sufficient confidence in herself. But he advised against marriage unless it was late in life "else it will bring later discouragements and discontent, even of a greater nature than exist at present."

This he traced directly to her former life in France, where she was the wife of a disgruntled physical bully who so resented the "beauty and affability of the Entity that he sought to keep her submerged, even at times using force." The weals on her body from his floggings were still vivid in her memory. "Hence the fear of punishment in the present, of being misunderstood or misinterpreted.

"The Entity then was a musician, but was cut short in same because of the association. Thus, in the present, the Entity will be required to determine what type of friendships with others she would like, then set about to plan them. . . . For they that make themselves friendly, have friends."

The Reading then described her life at the time of the Christian persecutions.

"The Entity accepted the teachings of the followers of Jesus; yet the torments of the persecutions became so abhorrent that the Entity became submerged in mere drudgery in order to keep away from the words, the hurts, the slights and slurs. . . .

"But know, as ye live in thy conscience in such good faith with thy Maker that ye can look every person in the face and know that ye have done naught but good in thought or deed, ye stand exalted before thy Maker. And if the Lord be on thy side, who can be against thee? . . .

"Before that, the Entity was in the Egyptian land, during those periods when there was the purifying of the body for active service in the Temples. The Entity then entered into a life of service, being what today would be called a nurse, one who cared for those physically or mentally ill.

"These phases can be a portion of the Entity's present experience or desire, unless timidity prevents the putting of same into practical application.

"As to the abilities of the Entity in the present: first find thyself and thy ideal, mentally, spiritually, physically, then apply same to thy relationships to others.

"Study music and apply same, either as the instructor or as the one giving the concert, or the like. For in that field ye will find harmony of life, harmony of expression, harmony of relationship to the Creative Forces. Ready for questions."

Jane: "Will I ever make close friends?"

E.C.: "If practiced in those things indicated, yes."

Jane: "What causes my absentmindedness?"

E.C.: "Self-condemnation! Do not condemn. Rather know, and live in self, that which we have indicated."

Jane: "What musical instruments should I take up?"

E.C.: "The piano as the basis, to be sure, but any stringed instruments."

Jane: "Is my mental ability and physical condition suitable to continue my college education?"

E.C.: "By all means! Continue such!"

Jane: "Why didn't I get in a sorority last February?"

E.C.: "Because of fear! As indicated, practice those things you would like others to do for you, by doing the same for others!"

Jane: "What is my I.Q.?"

E.C.: "This would depend on the standard by which it would be judged. It is sufficient for all your

> requirements, if ye will but apply self—first
> from the spiritual and mental, then from the
> material angle."
>
> Jane: "How can I overcome my intense fear—fear of
> meeting and conversing with other people?"
>
> E.C.: "As has been indicated!"

How much more simply and lucidly could constructive counsel be given to an inhibited girl, who, until
the time of her Reading, had no practical means of
resolving her own confusions!

Obviously no one in Jane's position could be expected to identify her fears with those of an ill-
treated wife whose spirit had been broken by the
sadism of a boorish lout. Yet, once she understood
the source of her social timidity, it had the effect of
exonerating the innocent people she had needlessly
been fearing, and enabling her to see them in an
objective, congenial light. Her confidence was being
taught to emerge like a baby being taught to walk.
How very clearly this illustrates Cayce's answer to:
"Why don't we remember past lives?"

"We do not have to remember," he said in effect.
"We are the sum total of all our memories." We
manifest them in our habits, our idiosyncracies, our
likes and dislikes, or talents and blind-spots, our
physical and emotional strengths and vulnerabilities.

Because of his life as Bainbridge, for example,
Edgar Cayce never had the slightest desire to gamble
or drink. The memory of the cost, the waste of
endeavor, was still too recent. This is why he insisted
that anyone with sufficient honesty to examine his
own nature, would find in it a complete lexicon of
do's and don't's . . . the still small voice of conscience
never lies. It is simply that we conveniently choose
not to hear it occasionally, and then wonder why we

walk slam-bang into a glass door that all but flattens our nose.

There is something infectious in Cayce's exuberance when he chaffs a soul for having relinquished self-confidence in the face of life's buffeting.

"You have belittled yourself and cramped your own abilities!" he exhorted a woman of forty-six. "Turn yourself loose! You may go anywhere so long as you keep your faith in the one God, and just apply self to being kind, patient, showing brotherly love.

"Too long have you been under a cloud, as it were, and rather timid and lacking in self-expression. You need to get out in the wilds and yell, and hear your own echo back again!

"Do not be subdued by others who try, or have tried, to impress you with their importance, for God is not a respecter of persons! And anyone can act the fool by appearing to be important!

"The greatest among those of the earth are those who serve the most; but this doesn't mean keeping so quiet, being so uncommunicative.

"There is a lack of flash and show. If you would dress up in a red dress, you could cut a nice caper, and this is not meant as a pun, either! Such urges have been so subdued, the love and deep emotion kept hid so long, that little of your real beauty has emerged.

"You need to change your environment, to be where you will meet lots of people and have to do a lot of talking, and a lot of explaining to people that you realize don't know nearly as much as you do.

"Give to those who think they know a lot! If you will only realize it, you know a lot more than they do, on any subject! These conditions, once changed, will make a great deal of difference to you. . . . So don't be afraid of having troubles; know that whatever you want, you can have. For the Lord loveth those who love Him, and He will not withhold any good thing from such!"

And in the same vein, he rallied a nervous young man of twenty: "Overcome timidity by having something particular to say! Many individuals talk without saying anything—that is, anything constructive or anything which even has meaning—but you take their opinions of you literally!

"We are given only two eyes, two ears, but we should hear and see twice—nay, four times—as much as we speak! Never be boastful, but never attempt to be 'just as the other boys, and do what people say lest you may be thought different.'

"Dare to be different! And if ye will begin with Deuteronomy, thirtieth chapter, and Exodus 19:5, you will know the reasons deep within self!"

CHAPTER SIX

VOCATIONAL KARMA

The following is an outstanding example of Cayce's encouragement earning him the undying friendship of the youth he helped.

John Schofield, aged twenty-three, suffered much early frustration in a dead-end mechanical job in a commercial engraving firm. This suffering was aggravated by a possessive family which allowed him no mind of his own. He was a fair-to-middling amateur artist in his own right, but lacked any confidence in his own creative worth. He had painted himself into a corner of the room, as it were, and the paint showed every sign of taking a long time to dry.

As many did, Schofield applied to Edgar Cayce as a last resort, all other sources of help having failed. He was briskly advised to put a healthy distance between himself and his parasitic family. In his past lives in Egypt, Greece and Rome he had many times been involved with the designing of frescoes for the temples, law courts and seats of government. This is

87

a highly specialized vocation, not confined to purely architectural skill, yet not as informal as mural painting. Nevertheless he was directed to go to New York and seek his place among the major architectural firms, once he had completed his vocational training at an art school.

Cayce explained that architectural styles in different lands were the sum total of the inspiration of the men who labored to create them over the centuries, even though their immediate rewards had been little more than their own dedication to their artistic ideals. He cited Leonardo da Vinci as an example of a genius whose soul was expressing itself, now in the present, as it had never been allowed to do in his own lifetime. The genius of da Vinci could only be expressed when the world had progressed sufficiently to recognize it and put his creations into practice. Thus his true immortality manifested itself in his universal influence, not in his personal fame.

The same argument applied to John Schofield's inborn talents.

"Why should this be?

"Because this soul, having gained so much in the decorative influence in the temples, in the public buildings, in the tombs, is now beginning its true career in America. And there may be seen in the decorative style of the frescoing, or second panels, in the Pantheon and its casements, influences which derived from the same school in which the Entity once studied."

"Just how should I prepare myself to contribute to this?" asked Schofield.

"By learning to combine the modernistic with the Phoenician and Egyptian, for they combine beautifully, their simplicity, their decorativeness."

Schofield proceeded as instructed, and five years later he was able to report on his progress.

"I received a sudden message to appear at the Barnes' Foundation, where I am a student, to be awarded a traveling scholarship for four months study in Europe with a group of his students this summer . . . from May 18 to September 18. It includes travel and instruction in seven countries.

"This year terminates my fifth and final year at the Academy of Fine Arts, and my second at the Barnes' Foundation. I am seeking new values and new inspiration for that ultimate course which I am to pursue.

"I feel very lucky and very grateful for the opportunities that have come to me. My sincere and humble wish is that I may prove deserving of them and develop an expression that is meaningful to those who seek an experience in art."

"My trip this summer was a wonderful series of experiences and I must have lived a lifetime in that period," he subsequently wrote to Hugh Lynn Cayce after Edgar's death. "Since my return I have been true to the Reading, and with much experimenting, have completed my first fresco, and am well along on planning my second. My first was rather successful, and my second one is hopeful. I have had a very good year, probably the best yet in the way of actual accomplishment."

Nine years later, Hugh Lynn Cayce was able to make the following appraisal:

"It is natural that we have watched with interest this young man's years of work and study in art school and his rise to remarkable heights in his field. Anyone who could compare the suppressed young man of a few years ago and the young scholar and artist whose work is being recognized today would see why we feel that the Life Readings are so worth studying."

THE INTELLIGENCE OFFICER

It is a far cry from Schofield to the complex soul who is involved in the next case history—too complex a soul to make full use of his Life Reading, even though it correctly foretold the how and the where of the role he would play in World War II.

Calvin Mortimer, Ph.D., was a psychologist, whose Reading defined him as "an extremist in some of his ideas," a soul who had returned for a very definite purpose, who possessed a well-developed talent for dealing with "very large groups of people in many varied spheres of activity.

"Before this, the Entity was in the land of the present nativity, during the period just following the American Revolution . . . among the soldiery of the British, acting in the American land in what would be termed the Intelligence Service. Not as a spy, but rather one of those who mapped and laid out the plans for the campaigns by Howe and Clinton.

"However, the Entity remained in the American soil after hostilities ended. Not as one dead, but as one making for the cooperation between the peoples of the Entity's native land and those of the land of adoption.

"Then in the name Warren, the Entity gained by successfully establishing these relationships.

"Hence, in the present, we will find diplomatic relationships, the exchange of ideas and plans of the various nations, becoming of interest to the Entity."

Before that, he had been an English Crusader who was taken prisoner by the Saracens in the Holy

Lands, and was profoundly impressed by the civilized handling he received from the "heathen infidel."

He lost in that life by uncritically defending a false cause rather than serving an ideal he genuinely believed in. This lent him a skepticism in the present towards religious or philosophic principles, though he retained his fascination for dogmas that can sway whole masses of people.

In a Persian incarnation before that, he lost again by indulging the carnal to excess, though he came under the influence of Esdras, of whom it was said: "According to tradition, all the writings of the Bible were destroyed, but they were restored by Esdras who 'remembered in his heart' and rewrote them."

He had also mastered the science of astronomy; "thus a knowledge of the movements of the earth are still a portion of the Entity's record."

In prehistoric Egypt "the Entity made for the greater progress in his development of the mental, or soul experiences. With the gathering of various races and creeds, the Entity made a study of same, classifying and interpreting them for the many, not only in the Egyptian land, but in the Indian, the Mongolian or Gobi, the Carpathian, and the Og, and those lands across the seas."

It is now possible to follow his destiny from the account supplied by his third ex-wife.

At the time of the bombing of Pearl Harbor "he was too old for active duty, and being a specialist in Public Opinion, he dashed off to Washington to see if he could be of use in this field.

"After a number of barren interviews, he came home discouraged, but it was not long before he had a new idea. Living on navigable water and having the means with which to indulge himself, he had considerable experience with sailboats, and so he applied to the Coast Guard.

"He passed the Navy I.Q. test with the score of 175, was slated to be a Lieutenant Commander, and came home to polish up on his navigation. Then he was urgently called back to Washington.

"Within a few months he was switched to the O.W.I. Domestic Intelligence Service as an Opinion Expert, where he worked closely with the O.S.S., and then with O.W.I. Overseas. He finished the war in charge of a technical school, training men to drop behind enemy lines, on the selfsame spot in Long Island where he had once mapped and laid out the plans for the campaigns of Howe and Clinton in the War of Independence."

In 1957 Dr. Mortimer married again for the fourth time. His third wife reported that her own marriage had lasted ten years, longer than any of the rest, presumably because they had been together before, harmoniously in Persia, and incompatibly as man and wife in the War of Independence.

In the latter years of their marriage he had insisted on too much drinking, and that she drink with him, "so that even now it is still quite a problem for me." She mentioned the terrific sex drive which had dominated their marriage.

She wrote again in 1963 to announce his death, during his sleep, after he had suffered two strokes and lost his sight.

She herself died very suddenly in the following year, having spoken of the "terrific pull" which she felt from him, "as if he were hypnotizing me to join him."

It is possible that, had Mortimer heeded Cayce's warnings against self-indulgence and excesses, he might have stuck to the very definite purpose for which he returned. This presumably was a continuation of the advance he had begun to make in Egypt at a high responsible level of international diplomacy.

But Mortimer's nostalgic appetite for the erotic fleshpots of Persia proved an insurmountable obstacle.

It is not out of keeping here to consider the Oriental belief that the soul is allowed one "comfortable" reincarnation for every six lives of arduous development, the theory being that the lives grow correspondingly tougher as the soul sheds the ties that bind it to earth. Without this "sabbatical," the soul might well weary of the constant upward struggle and allow itself to become unduly discouraged.

By this same token, it could be possible that the Mortimers had reached the sixth life of such a cycle, and that Dr. Mortimer and his wife will return next time to a more tranquil existence, where they can put their house in order and assess their spiritual progress more clearly.

CHAPTER SEVEN

LIFE READINGS FOR CHILDREN

Whenever Edgar Cayce was dealing with children, his loving concern was detectable even in the flat pages of the transcripts.

In ordinary life, children were drawn to him instinctively. In his time, he had been a most successful children's photographer, due to the magical rapport he was able to establish between his young sitters and himself.

From as far back as the turn of the century, he had taught Sunday School, and his pupils kept in affectionate touch with him long after they went out into the world.

THE DOCTOR IN SPITE OF HIMSELF

Roddy was born at 4:43 a.m. January 9, 1943, and his parents requested his Reading the following June.

"As will be seen, in the not too distant future," the Reading begins, "all those souls who enter the earth plane in the years '43, '44 and '45 will apparently be destined to fulfill interesting roles in their service to their fellow man, and find a very unusual approach to same.

"This Entity, if given the opportunity in its early environs, is destined to be a professional man in this experience, preferably in the fields of medicine, or dentistry, or as a pharmacist. Any of these will be channels through which the Entity may attain the fulfillment of his purpose.

"As the Entity develops, it will be seen that he will have a great imagination. Do not rebuke the Entity for telling 'tall tales,' for, to the Entity, they will be true. Just impress on him how these may be used more constructively in the application of self towards spiritual, mental and material unfoldments.

"He will be inclined to be extravagant in his words, in his attitudes. This, too, will need to be—not curbed by 'you can't do this,' or 'you can't do that,' but by encouraging him in other interests that will create in him a constant appreciation of being consistent, in that he 'does as well as he speaks.'

"Astrologically we find Venus, Mercury, Mars and Jupiter as influences. In Venus we find the love of the beautiful.

"This will make for the determination that everything he attempts, if he is directed well, will be well done. And it will require patience on the part of those responsible for the Entity!

"We find in Mercury the high mental abilities. In Mars with Mercury we find quite a busybody, not inclined to interfere with others, but wanting to have his own way, and knowing how to do things just a little bit better than anyone else!

"We will find in Jupiter, as the unfoldments come, the greater universal consciousness, giving the abilities which were expressed by the same Entity in a previous experience as Harvey—Dr. Harvey, discoverer of the circulation of the blood.

"Though proven to be in error in many things, he still insisted, even then, that he knew best! His activities are well known, and, if studied, will give those responsible for the Entity an idea of the problems to be met.

"But do give the Entity the opportunity to study, either as a pharmacist, or as a dentist, and he will do the rest himself as he goes along."

Here indeed is a very big fish in a very small five-month-old pond!

In France, at the time of Cardinal Richelieu, the Entity had been "Count Dubourse, and had made great contributions to the advance of cleanliness in relationship to disease. Though the Entity made no pretenses, yet he indicated to others he knew better than they did. (And in that instance he did!) Especially in relation to diseases commonly called the "catching" diseases, for he insisted that these came not only from microbes but could be carried by individuals.

"Thus, in the present experience, it will be found that the Entity will be inclined to be clean about its person, though 'messy' about a house. These were the natural extremes indicated in the characteristics in that former experience, and will find expression in the present.

"And the Entity will be one of those who keeps his friends quite separate!

"Then, in the guidance you give him, do keep the spiritual life balanced with the purposeful life. And, as a normal balance is kept, we will find those abilities manifesting themselves in a way and measure as to bring blessings to many people."

When Edgar declared himself ready to answer questions, the mother asked when and where she had been associated with her boy in the past. The answer: "In many places—especially in Egypt as a directing influence. Thus care should be taken that not too great a disagreement ever arises between the two!"

The father had been with the boy in the French experience, "as well as in the Egyptian—where we find them in opposition to one another. So, expect a good many spats between 'em!"

Though this was of sad necessity the only Reading the child was ever to obtain, his mother made the following report to the A.R.E. ten years later.

"Roddy has shown particular interest in the physical body since a tiny child, and especially anything having to do with the heart and the circulation of the blood. He also definitely has the trait of insisting he is always right! He never wants to admit that another's explanation of anything is better than his. Has been an A-1 student; boasts of having had better grades than anyone else in school. Has a mind that researches into knowledge along whatever line he gets started. Has a phobia about germs—washes his hands all the time—definitely 'hipped' on the subject. Doesn't want to live in a big city because of 'all those people breathing germs on you'!

"Although we have never discussed his Reading with him, he insists he's going to be a doctor. At ten years old, he has his own paper route and is saving money towards medical college.

"We have four other children, all entirely different. These traits are definitely peculiar to this one child, just as Mr. Cayce stated when he was five months old. . . ."

All the eccentricities Edgar had foreseen in the baby had fully developed in less than ten years. Edgar indicated but never insisted on the course a child should follow. The responsibility lay directly with the parents as to whether they would encourage the child's medical ambitions or direct them into other channels. But at least they knew where his own instinctive proclivities lay, and why they were there.

THE PURITY OF A CHILD'S SOUL

In the files of children's case histories many are simple, unassuming human documents. The children often face uneventful destinies in quiet obscurity, the problems are not major or dramatic. But every so often one emerges with such unique overtones that it deserves inclusion for its human interest alone.

One young "original," aged three, received this Life Reading in 1936:

"Much crowds in to be said!" Edgar began, "for the Entity is very sensitive, very high-strung, inclined to be very stubborn, and very expressive of feeling. . . . For the Entity is an old soul, and an Atlantean who, properly guided and directed, may not only make for his own development but make his surroundings, his environs, his world, a much better place for others.

"It will be found that few people will appear as strangers to the Entity, yet some will remain strangers ever, no matter how often or in what manner they are thrown together! The Entity will ever be tending towards an idealistic nature. Hence, unless it be made clear to the Entity as to why there will be faults and failures in the promises made by individuals and associates, he will tend to lose confidence, not only in others, but in self.

"And the loneliest person, the loneliest individual, yea the loneliest Entity, is the one who has lost hold upon his own self!"

In his previous life this Entity had been a gold miner in California who had become disgusted by the lawlessness and violence which had robbed him of his just rewards and brought him a violent death. Thus the child had inherited a terror of firearms, and they were never to be allowed in his presence. "Such explosions are fearful experiences to the Entity.

"But the Entity never lost hold upon self . . . and if asked in the present: 'Can you do this or that?' he will always answer that he can 'if you show him how!'

"He will ever seek new fields of activity, for everything about the Entity must be new. Hence a word of counsel to those who aid the Entity in the formative years: do not be overawed or surprised when he informs those about him that they are 'out of date'l"

The Entity had been an imposing figure in Roman times, a wealthy and influential supervisor of the collection of tithes and taxes, and during the final inundations of Atlantis, he had been a key official in the directing of refugees to resettlements in Egypt, the Pyrenees and Central and South America. In the present, "law should be the vocation," preferably international law.

His father was an old friend who had been with him through the disillusion of the gold fields, and again in Egypt at the time of the Exodus. And in that same incarnation his mother had been his daughter . . . "hence there will arise periods in the present when the son will doubt his own parents' authorityl"

There were obviously stormy days ahead, but Cayce was confident that as long as the parents always explained why they expected a high standard of conduct from him, he would understand and obey.

This Reading is absolutely unique in the following respect. Cayce, having consulted the boy's Akashic Record, made this aside during the session: "The cleanest record I've ever experienced. The book is the cleanest. And yet I had never thought of any of them not being perfectly clean before."

Frederick Leighton was five months old when Edgar Cayce gave him a Life Reading in 1931. He commented on an as yet unformed character (which is unusual in itself), thus placing the responsibility for the child's development squarely on the shoulders of the parents. Not until the second half of his life would the inner characteristics from his previous lives begin to manifest. He would have a natural affinity for music, having been an itinerant entertainer or "barnstormer" in the south and southwest just after the cessation of the War Between the States, and he had brought with him a predilection for folk songs.

He would develop a talent for business and law "but not confining same in a closed space such as a store, office or the like. Rather will he tend to express himself in the open, in the crowd, on the stage, or as the political leader or speaker." A strong religious influence was traced back to a life in Jerusalem as a harpist in the temple. In ancient Egypt he had again dedicated his life to music, as well as becoming rich "by service to many in the distributing of food from the royal granaries. (Thus) we will find in the latter portion of the present, the Entity will accumulate much of the word's goods from the world's storehouse."

Then came a warning to the parents: "As to whether the Entity becomes one broken in will, broken in its ability to think, to recall much from the spiritual side of its life, depends on what is trained in or trained out by those in authority in the formative years." Otherwise the child was assured of a fully rounded and successful life, either in politics or music.

The implied warnings were not without foundation. When Frederick was four, he suffered a major accident to his head. Allowed to play with a pair of scissors, he stabbed them into his right eye, narrowly avoiding permanent damage to his frontal brain. An immediate operation was performed, but he developed a cataract, and his sight was endangered.

As a result of the seven Physical Readings obtained for him in the next two years, he regained his sight. His grateful response to this is conveyed in this excerpt from a report: "And in walking down the road with little Frederick, I found that he loves Mr. Cayce as far as the stars. . . ."

A TRIPLE DEBT

Sarah Crothers was thirteen when her parents belatedly requested a Life Reading for her. For some time Edgar Cayce had been supplying Physical Readings to counter the particularly stubborn case of epilepsy which had plagued her since birth. Under the Physical Readings she would make progress and then slip back. Possibly the Readings were incorrectly applied, or the parents had to deal with doctors hostile to the unorthodox diagnoses. No othe~ explanation offered itself until Edgar got right to the heart of the matter in the opening paragraphs of the Life Reading.

He stated flatly that if the karmic records were to be of any use, the parents would have to shoulder their own share of the responsibility.

"Those responsible for this Entity, who oft are inclined to pass off the epileptic attacks as chance, or as conditions that are unavoidable, should parallel their obligations to her. For, with such a paralleling (through their own Life Readings, you see), there would be a much greater comprehension of the . . . self-aggrandizements or indulgences that now find expression in the physical condition of the Entity, who also is reaping her own whirlwind."

As a very young girl during the American Revolution, she had been used by her parents as a spy against her own countrymen, for the parents were afraid that the defeat of England would bring them financial ruin.

The girl was then called Marjorie Desmond, and possessed a certain amount of latent psychic ability that neither she nor her parents properly comprehended. Her father encouraged her to channel this energy into alluring susceptible young officers into sexual indiscretions, and "she excited the fires of the physical in many." The karmic crime was not so much the treachery to the young colony as the dangerous harnessing of psychic energy to sexual practices for sordid gain, and Edgar made no bones about placing equal blame on the parents. The child herself, however, had blundered twice before—in both lives she had been a Levite—and resentment and rebellion had left their imprint on her character.

"Before that, the Entity was in the Egyptian land, among the offspring of the Atlanteans, though born and reared in Egypt for the (purpose of serving in) what is now known as the hospitalization of individuals ill of body or mind."

Here one may suspect that her neglect or indifference caused the first fissures in the fabric of the soul, though Edgar Cayce, with his usual discretion, made no direct implication.

When he answered the parents' questions at the close of the session, he pointed to no easy solution.

Q.: "Has the condition of the body for the past

ten years had any effect upon it physically and mentally?"

E.C.: "Necessarily, these have not been—nor are they yet—coordinated."

Q.:"What type of education should she have to prepare her for life?"

E.C.: "The musical education, as well as the encouragement towards nursing."

Q.: "What effect has destiny on the present appearance?"

E.C.: "This depends, as indicated, upon the application of those who have brought the Entity into its present environ. The gain will be according to how well the obligations due the Entity are met."

Q.: "What will aid her to overcome her physical and mental ailments?"

E.C.: "As indicated—physical exertion, exercises and activities for the body."

It is difficult to ignore the subconscious reluctance implicit in the father's subsequent correspondence, and at the end of the voluminous file on this case, one is left with the regretful impression that the child's progress was minimal, and the karmic debt by no means expunged.

THE BUBBLE REPUTATION

This seems an opportune moment to point out that the "celebrities" of history represent a very small minority in the Life Readings. Cayce suggested that most souls made their greatest spiritual advances while living obscure and uneventful lives, usually under fairly straightened circumstances. The serf and the peasant had few pleasures and many burdens until the middle of this century. Nevertheless, the average initiate to reincarnation toys rather wistfully with the possibility that he has, at least once, caused the earth to bow down before him.

Unfortunately, it matters very little how important you once were, and very much that you are conforming to decent standards in the immediate present.

Alexander Hamilton (1775-1804), soldier-hero and a founding father of the American Constitution, whose life was cut short by the famous duel, would seem to have been a highly-evolved soul at a mature level of unselfish dedication. Yet this did not prevent him returning as a rather harassed young man of the Jewish faith whose parents obtained his first Reading from Edgar Cayce when he was five weeks old.

Edgar Cayce at once warned against an erratic temper that could cause trouble in later years, and emphasized that the boy should be protected from tampering with firearms. The Entity had brought with him no preconceived pattern of soul development; this he would have to develop as he grew. He was advised to study "in law and in the financial forces and principles of the land."

Before the boy was five, his father fell in love with another woman; the parents were divorced, and the mother retained custody of the child. (Broken homes were always somber hazards to Edgar Cayce. He put intense emphasis on the need of every soul to have a secure background during its formative years, and maintained that the preservation of a congenial home was the highest achievement that a soul could aim for in terms of its own progression.)

At the age of twenty-five, the young man was displaying "a very dogmatic attitude about life in general," which a year and a half in the Navy had failed to cut down to size.

The following year found him under psychiatric care and in hospital for shock treatments. His innate tendency to violence had caught up with him. Having met every conflict head-on, he had added to his problems by an impulsive marriage to a divorcee with a child. The repercussions of the broken home revealed themselves here, in that the girl who had broken up his father's marriage and the girl he himself married were of the same ethnic origin, had the same red hair and were both wives of men laboring in the same mechanical field.

When the marriage only served to compound his miseries, he began to suffer belated remorse that he had not kept on friendlier terms with his father during his lifetime. Towards the end of the following year he seemed to feel his only hope of salvaging himself lay in becoming a rabbi, but a further attempt to contact him by the A.R.E. resulted in the return of the letter marked "Address Unknown."

From his Life Reading, one tends to assume that the bad debts accrued in an earlier Greek life had taken precedence over the gains he had made as Hamilton. Elsewhere in the Readings, the Trojan War gives evidence of having roused sufficient violence in many of its protagonists to deter and confuse their subsequent soul-development. Being in essence a civil war, the passions generated by this war bit deep enough for their scars to reach down the centuries. Using the average patterns of the Readings as a yardstick, this unhappy young man will need yet another life to expunge from his own karmic records the ugly warp left by the Trojan War.

What is most illuminating in the study of this case history is the fact that, as Alexander Hamilton, he had been able to rise to the occasion when his aid was urgently needed by this young nation in crisis. He had been able to come to his task stripped for creative action. All his negatives had been left in abeyance against a future day, when he could apply himself to them in a more settled and resolved period of his country's history. This alone denotes a basic selfless-ness struggling to express itself in the soul. In which case, he has justly earned and justly deserves the al-truistic prayers of his fellow men for his ultimate wel-fare—as long as they are couched in terms of "prayer for the living" and not "prayer for the departed."

THE MEMORY OF THE MASTER

The Readings leave one in no doubt that the most permanent benediction that a soul can bring with it to its lives on earth is the memory of a blessing bestowed on it by Jesus himself.

In one instance a little girl of five would never say her prayers unless her mother stood beside her with her hand on her head, symbolizing in the present the reassuring touch of the Master's hand when he blessed her as a child in the Holy Land.

And when Edgar gave a Reading for another one-year-old child in 1935, he laid special emphasis on the fact that "during the period when the Master walked in the earth, the Entity was among those children who were blessed by Him on the way from Bethany.

"The Entity then beheld and knew Him as one who drew children to Him, and heard that spoken by Him: 'Lest ye become as little children, ye will in no wise enter in.'

"For if one would be forgiven as a child, one must forgive those who would err against self.

"Then the Entity was of the household of Cleopas, in the name Clementina," and in her early teens, hav-ing followed the training of the disciples to follow in His steps, attached herself in service to Mark and Luke during their journeying across the land, becom-ing so closely associated with Mark as to aid in the preservation of "those lessons as we find in the gospel recorded by Mark."

Thus her parents were urged to encourage the child's memories as Clementina, for her present life would be best expressed in unselfish service to others.

CHILD CARE

The A.R.E. files contain an abundance of grateful correspondence from people Cayce helped physically and spiritually. But none are more affecting than the letters from parents of children too young to understand the source of their help.

His views on upbringing consistently emphasized the need for absolute honesty with the child. He condemned pampering as firmly as he condemned insecurity and lack of self-esteem left it susceptible to and understanding entered life with serious limitations. Without a secure and solid background, a child's insecurity and lack of self-esteem left it susceptible to the negative habit-patterns of the faults and woes of its previous lives. Cayce urged the parent always to explain the reason for proper discipline, never to apply it autocratically "because I say so." By always appealing to the child's faculty for reasoning, a stable foundation could be laid for its character. When Cayce came across indifference or lack of affection in a parent, he had no hesitation in saying so bluntly. Nothing disturbed him more than the parent who tried to force his own fears and prejudices down the throat of the young soul entrusted to his keeping. The source of most neuroses in later life was this "force-feeding" in childhood of illogical do's and don'ts, as if the child were merely a puppet-extension of its parents' repressions and frustrations.

Cayce constantly urged that the encouragement of

the best in a child was a twenty-four-hour job, and must be done gladly, never as a chore. The child must be reasoned away from its own weaker characteristics, not bribed away, or made to feel unduly conscious of them. Religion should be presented in its most benign and spiritual aspects, free of any intolerance or coercion. The development of a good sense of humor was essential to the balance and perspective in adulthood. Any inclination towards music should be warmly stimulated because of its harmonious aid to the child's growing self-awareness. "Just as exercise for the hands and arms, music used for creative purposes is helpful. Through music, you may find the greatest expression of self."

In answer to a mother's question: "How can the mother best cope with this temperament for the best development?" Edgar Cayce replied: "It isn't so much 'cope with it' as just meet it! Be just as patient as you would like thy child to be. The child will then be more patient with you also."

"What course of studies should she pursue in secondary and higher education?"

"Music! History of, the activity of, all of its various forms. If you learn music, you'll learn history! If you learn music you'll learn mathematics! If you learn music, you'll learn all there is to learn—unless it's something bad!"

CHILDREN IN WARTIME

Towards the close of his life, as World War II loomed darker and darker, Edgar Cayce's concern for the children who would be innocently caught in its meshes became more and more evident and urgent. He was not alone in the fear that the souls of children, bewildered by violent deaths, would wander in equal bewilderment in the lower astral planes, unable to proceed 'towards the Light,' and that they would tend in their confusion to return to earth too swiftly, merely for the sake of the temporary sanctuary of a womb. Joan Grant, the English psychic, was equally concerned, and her psychiatrist husband, Denys Kelsey, using the regression technique in hypnosis, came across many cases of these "war children" reincarnating too soon, into uncongenial families, in search of makeshift shelter from the terrors of the bombing and extermination camps which had clung to them like malignant thought-forms after death.

Fletcher, the spirit-guide of the psychic Arthur Ford, had taken care never to reincarnate after his death on a Flanders battlefield in World War I. He was then a young French Canadian soldier of seventeen. He is an "original," in that he is perfectly happy on the plane he inhabits for the time being, a cheerful, gregarious sprite with more *joie de vivre* than many of the people who come to Arthur Ford to consult him.

The first poignant chord struck in the Readings occurred in August, 1943, when Edgar was asked by the distressed mother of a four-year-old girl to account for her nightmares and constant terror of city life.

Edgar discreetly refrained from overstressing the soul's previous lives; advising the mother to wait until the girl was in her eleventh year before requesting a second Life Reading. (This sometimes forewarned of a potential tragedy or even an early death.)

"For here we have a quick return to earth," he observed, "from fear, back to fear, through fear." He counsels that the child must be protected from all "loud noises, darkness, the scream of sirens."

"For (in her previous life) the Entity was only just coming to that awareness of the beauty of associations, of friendships, of the beautiful outdoors, flowers, birds, and of God's manifestations to man of the beauty, of the oneness of purpose in nature itself, when the tramping of feet, the shouts and rattle of arms, brought destructive forces.

The child had then been only a year or two years older than she is now, he explained, thus the past and present were inextricably interlocked in her mind, and she could not distinguish between the ordinary din of New York city and the Nazi hooliganism that had shattered her world and brought about her death.

"The Entity then, in the name Theresa Schwalendal, lived on the border of Lorraine and Germany. The Entity had no sooner passed on then she reentered the material world in less than nine months.

"Be patient. Do not scold. Do not speak harshly. Do not fret nor condemn the body-mind. But *do* tell her daily of the love that Jesus had for little children, of peace and harmony. Never tell her those stories of witches, never those of fearfulness, of any great punishment, only those of love, patience.

"Do this, and we will find a great, a wonderful soul, that has come again to bless many.

"We are through for the present."

THE KING'S JESTER

Edgar's hesitancy to detail the future prospects of a doomed child is again evident when he gives this Reading in 1944 for a seven-year-old boy living in London, England, during the Battle of Britain.

"Thus we would confine the direction to the training, the counseling. And then, when the Entity has reached that period of his own choice, or, at thirteen years of age, we would give further directions, if these are sought by the Entity himself.

"With all the horrors of destruction, with all the trials in the minds of men in this period through which this Entity and his associates in his early experiences are passing, *do* keep alive in him the ability to see not only the sublime things of life, but the humor, the wit—yes, the ridiculous also—that may be drawn from the cynic as well as the pessimist, as in cartoons and the like. For the Entity should be trained in the abilities as a writer, using historical facts as the background of such writings . . . for in the experience before this, the Entity was a jester in the Court of England, in the name of Hockersmith . . . and set many things in order, when there were those great stresses owing to the selfishness of men.

"Also the Entity was among those peoples of Israel who entered the Holy Land, who were married to the Canaanites. Yet the Entity was not among those who led the children of Israel astray. For he forsook Astheroth and served rather the God of Abraham, Isaac and Jacob, as did the one who led the children of Israel through the Red Sea, across the Jordan.

"But when the Entity is thirteen years, we would give further directions.

"Train him especially in English, and at Eton.

"We are through with this reading."

This letter from the mother, written to Hugh Lynn Cayce in February, 1947, confirms Edgar's concern.

"My son passed quickly into the other plane of consciousness at about 4:30 p.m. on February 6. I am in the hospital today, expecting my third child. Timmy was looking forward eagerly to 'his' arrival and was most anxious he should be a boy. He also said, a few weeks before he died: 'I'd like you to be my Mummy in my next life.' I told him he might not be able to arrange that, but he persisted; 'I'm going

112

to ask God anyway.' I remember answering, 'Well, there is no harm in asking."' I feel he was well prepared for what we call 'death.' I had told him, in resumé, the story in *There Is a River*, and before that I had simplified for him Stewart Edward White's *The Unobstructed Universe*.

"My first thought was that he would come back to us in the body of this tiny baby, especially as I had felt and told my husband that I felt that this baby had no personality as yet, and I wondered what type of soul we would attract this time. . . . I do not, however, now feel that he necessarily will choose to return so soon, even though he 'would like me to be his Mummy in his next life.'

"It may be too soon; there may be things for him to learn on another plane of consciousness. It may also be too much the same situation, which was unsettling to him. He (this is hard to explain in a few words) was sensitive to the chaos in the world, and to the financial insecurity of the last two years which we have had due to his father's generosity and kindness to his mother, who died 1/23/47 after living with us as a helpless invalid . . . I had to neglect my children to nurse her at a time when I was pregnant. It was all too much for me, and Timmy suffered with me and for his father, who was at a loss what to do about it, and was consequently impatient and nervous, and not his usual loving, cheerful self; so that the loving, happy atmosphere of our home was completely destroyed from about August '46 until 3/26/47, when I feel Timmy succeeded in restoring it with our cooperation. He always was most solicitous that his Daddy and Mummy should be united and loving, as we were, except when our house became the home of either my family or his, even if only for a visit of a few months. . . ."

She enclosed a newspaper clipping which described how Timmy and a friend had "ventured onto a frozen pond; the ice broke and they disappeared together. Death was due in both cases to shock. . . ."

In his answering letter of sympathy, Hugh Lynn Cayce made the following comment: "I wonder if you realize that his Life Reading was unusually short, and that there was a reticence about giving any information until he could ask for himself. I think there is much that we must come to understand regarding the interrelation between this plane of consciousness and those on the other side of the state we call death. Perhaps Timmy can get his Reading now, and go on preparing for the work which the Reading indicated he could accomplish. . . ."

THE CALL OF THE SEA

At the age of seventeen, Fred Coe terminated an adolescence of restriction and incompatibility by running away from home. Two months later he was still missing, and Edgar Cayce was requested to trace him. The Reading, though brief, is as intriguing as any, telling its own story with lucid economy and vigor.

"Yes, we have the Entity here," Edgar began. "In entering the earth plane, we find he comes under the influence of Neptune and Uranus, with influences from Jupiter and Mars. Hence the condition exhibited in the present is a love of the sea. (See? The body has gone to sea).

"In the planetary influence then, we find one of many exceptional abilities.

"One who is considered eccentric and peculiar, having many changeable moods.

"One loving mystery tales of the sleuth or detective

114

order, and every condition regarding a mystery of the sea.

"One who should have been guided close in the study of those things pertaining to the mystery and the occult.

"One who will find his greatest abilities in the present earth's plane in the study of the occult forces.

"One who loves the use of firearms, and likes the display of same.

"One that in the present year finds the greatest change coming in the life, when he will find many experiences in many lands, returning only to the present surroundings of birth in middle age.

"One who finds little need for that called a religious life.

"One who will bring much joy and much sorrow to many, especially to the weaker sex.

"One with the ability to give much counsel to many.

"In the previous appearances, we find many of the various urges influencing the present existence. In the existence before this, we find the Entity often referred to as Captain Kidd. The Entity gained in the first portion of the life, and in the latter portion gave much to others, though the cost to self was rather severe. In the urge is found the love of the sea, of those things which pertain to the mysterious, the ability to gain mystery in the eyes of others.

"In the life before that, we find the Entity known as Hawk, in the English navy. The Entity then was aide to the first of the navigators to the eastern portion of the world (John Cabot, 1497); and in the latter days came to the northern shore of this land.

"The urge, again, is the love of adventure and of mystery.

"In the life before that, we find him in that land of the Bedouins, when the war was made between the then Grecian forces and the peoples of the plain (circa 900 B.C.). The Entity then was in the name Xenia, and was the second-in-command of those plainsmen who brought consternation to the invading forces by turning hornets loose among them! That life, as we see, brought power to the Entity, and in the end proved his undoing. Here is seen the present love of outdoors and the mysteries of nature.

"In the life before that (circa 10,000 B.C.) in that period when there were divisions in the land now known as Egypt, the Entity wrought then in iron, in the service of the ruler. And in that service brought much counsel to many. The urge in the present—a desire to be of service to, and in direct communication with, those in power.

"Many, many, developments will be necessary before this Entity attains oneness with the higher forces. Study, then, those conditions; and let those who would assist, take warning.

"We are through for the present."

This is one case where his sympathies were clearly with the boy and not with the parents; and when they requested a second reading, the only information Edgar would vouchsafe was that the boy had shipped aboard a seagoing vessel in New York, eastward bound for Europe.

In the next case, however, one is suddenly pulled up short by the jolt of stark tragedy.

THE GRAPES OF WRATH

The mother of a twelve-year-old boy, Lennie Talbot, asked for her son's Life Reading in the hope that it would aid her to understand his mercurial behavior-pattern.

Despite the great tact Edgar always employed, the

116

Reading clearly reveals his serious concern for the boy's future welfare, and a note of sober warning is implicit in every line.

"In giving the records here of this Entity, it would be easy to interpret them either in a very optimistic or a very pessimistic vein. For there are great possibilities and great obstacles. Here is the opportunity for an Entity (while comparisons are odious, these would be good comparisons) to be either a Beethoven or a Whittier; or a Jesse James! For the Entity is inclined to think more highly of himself than he ought; and that is what these three individuals did. As to the application made of it, this depends upon the individual self.

"Here is an Entity who has abilities latent within self which may be turned into music, or poetry, or writing in prose which few would ever excel. Or there may be the desire to have his own way to such an extent that he will disregard others altogether, in every form, just so he has his own way.

"In giving the astrological aspects, these are latent and manifested: Mercury, Venus, Jupiter, Saturn and Mars. These are adverse in some respects, one to another, yet are ever present, and indicate that the body will go to excess in many ways, unless there is real training in the period of unfoldment. And the Entity is beginning to reach that period when—while the spirit must not be broken!—everyone should be very firm and positive, inducing him through reason to analyze himself, and to form a proper concept of his ideals and purposes, and in doing this, we will not only give to the world a real individual with genius, but make for proper soul development. Otherwise, we will give to the world one with a genius for making trouble for somebody!

"As to the previous appearances in the earth, these

naturally—as indicated from those tendencies—have been quite varied:

"Before this, the Entity was in the present land during the French and Indian wars.

"The Entity was among the French in the activities about Fort Dearborn, determined to have his own way, irrespective of the trouble or the great distress he caused others.

"In the end, the Entity by sheer illness gained a great deal. For it may be said of this Entity, as of the Master, through suffering he learned the more.

"The name then was John Angel.

"Before that, the Entity was in what is now known as France.

"Then the Entity, with certain groups, made forays into the Hun land, and yet eventually escaped to the southern portion of Italy.

"The Entity was then of a disposition in which artistic or musical talents came into greater play, the ability to write verse and compose music to it.

"The ability to become an orchestra leader or a writer of song or verse may be a part of the Entity's experience in the present, provided he doesn't have the 'big head,' or think more highly of himself than he ought. Every other individual has as much right in the earth as you have yourself, even though he may not be in some respects as far advanced in his learning. God is not a respecter of persons because of their good looks or abilities. He respects the individual according to his purposes, his aims, his desires. Remember that.

"Before that, the Entity was in the City of Gold, during the early evolution of the various lands of Saad, the Gobi and Egypt (10,000 B.C.).

"The Entity was among those who acted as guards to the ladies in waiting, and was active in his ability to entertain in verse and in song, using these not only to entertain, but to aid the greater development and unfoldment of those people.

"Before that the Entity was in Atlantis, during those periods just before the second breaking up of the land (28,000 B.C.).

"The Entity was among the Sons of Belial who used the divine forces for the gratifying of selfish appetites, and the formation of this desire to gratify self became the stumbling block.

"As to the abilities of the Entity in the present, these are unlimited. How will they be directed by the Entity? How well may others aid the Entity to become aware of such activities? These questions should be put to self.

"Study first to know thy ideals, spiritual, mental and material. Then apply self towards these in such a manner that there will never be a question mark after thine own conscience nor in the eyes of others.

"Ready for questions."

Q: What should be his chief work?

E.C.: "This depends upon what he chooses—whether in directing of music, writing of music, or writing of verse—any of those are the realms through which the Entity may *exceed* as well as succeed."

Q: Should all of his talents be developed?

E.C.: "All his talents will either be developed, or run to seed and be drained off."

Q: Any other suggestions that may help his parents to guide him?

E.C.: "Let the parents study to show themselves approved unto God, workmen not ashamed, putting the stress where stress is due, keeping self unspotted from the world.

"We are through with this reading."

The Atlantean Sons of Belial will be dealt with in

the following chapter. For the moment, the reader may assume that this was the worst blot on his record, and the long-delayed karma which demanded its reckoning from this boy in the present had its ill-omened beginning in this period.

Excerpt I from the correspondence of the mother, February, 1944:

"Your reading for Lennie was no surprise to my husband and me. We early saw that such tremendous energy should be set to work, and he is in his third year at a very strict, very religious boarding school. Idleness would destroy him. He must always be in the big world, where he will be just a 'drop in the bucket,' not the 'big frog in a small pond'...."

Excerpt II, September, 1949:

"We are in great distress now over the condition of our only child, who has a distressing mental and nervous upset which as yet has not been diagnosed. ..."

Excerpt III, July, 1951, to Hugh Lynn Cayce:

"The press has been cruel to us in our sorrow, and no doubt you have read of our tragedy. My son Lennie, who has been emotionally unbalanced for three years, last Wednesday shot his grandfather and grandmother.

"Hugh Lynn, your father was my friend, and I brought Lennie to see him and also he gave a Life Reading for him which had plenty of warnings in it. I am writing to ask you to please get one of your prayer circles to work for us. ..."

Excerpt IV, August, 1951:

"Lennie is now in the State Hospital. The doctors there, and elsewhere in other sanitariums where he has been, have, of course, labeled his trouble dementia praecox, schizophrenia, etc., but you and I know it is bad karma. Thank God his intellect seems intact, he writes for books he has always liked, and he takes two newspapers. . . ."

Excerpt V, October, 1951:

"My husband and I have arranged to send him to a psychiatrist, Dr. Baker. He is very fine, one of the pioneers in insulin and electric shock treatment. I see no reason why Lennie should not receive osteopathic treatment while under Dr. Baker. He tells me that he will keep Lennie for a whole month for observation before he gives him any treatment, and I am going to urge that in this month he be given osteopathy. With our love and thanks again. . . ."

Excerpt VI, November, 1951:

"(This is Lennie's last letter. Please return to me)

"Dear Mother: I was indeed glad to hear about your trip through the Middle West, but have not yet heard about the results.

"I certainly feel better since Brother Lindsay prayed for me, and am less tense and worried about the future than before.

"Will you please take me to a healing revival? I could probably benefit from this more than from any other form of treatment. Do please find out where one is being held and let's go to it.

"Could you please send me my tweed suit and those new shoes which I wasn't allowed to wear at the other place. I could certainly use them here, as certain regulations are much more lenient.

"Also I would like my wrist watch, which I am also allowed. Please tell Father to buy me some canned goods and delicacies from the food market. All these items are very useful and they would come in very handy around here.

"You probably have not yet felt this year's tax increases, but your '52 income tax will be higher, leaving you less money to live on if you don't do any tax dodging. Business property, however, yields about the highest income after taxes for any investment.

"Love, Lennie."

Excerpt VII, June 1956:

"Miss (Gladys) Davis recommended Hildreth Sanitarium as being one that Mr. Cayce approved of, and for two years Lennie has been there. This is the only place where he has been content, and we think it the very best, regardless of price. Lennie, with only one setback, has steadily improved there, and we have great hopes that he will ultimately recover . . ."

These cases, more than any other type, serve to emphasize that Edgar Cayce viewed the future in two quite separate ways. While the personal destiny awaiting a given soul may consist of the inevitable consequences of his own past actions (and thus lend itself to psychic predetermination) the future can never be entirely preordained. A given country, for example, has the power to alter and reshape its destiny in exact accord with the altering behavior patterns of that people of that country. A stronger, more determined effort on the part of the responsible German majority could easily have prevented Hitler's rise to power. Europe could have followed a saner, more serene evolution. The earthquakes which threaten in California and South America can likewise be averted by a swing away from materiality and social indifference on the part of their inhabitants.

Cayce never put it more clearly than he did in one of his lectures, given in his normal conscious state to an A.R.E. prayer group.

"A warning was once given to a man of God that a certain city would be destroyed," he said. "But the man talked with God face to face, and God promised that if there were fifty righteous men, he would save it . . . then, finally, if there were just ten righteous men, He would spare the city.

"I believe that the just people in the world keep it going. The just people are the ones who have been kind to the other fellow . . . in patience, long-suffering, brotherly love, preferring their neighbor before themselves.

"When there are possibly fifty—or a hundred, or a thousand, or a million—then the way may well have been prepared for His coming.

"But all these just men must be united in their desire and supplication that the Christ physically walk among men again."

CHAPTER EIGHT

MAN—THE STRANGER IN THE EARTH

It might be good to call a halt here, while we recap Edgar Cayce's reasons for placing in God the only power to alleviate the soul's mortification when it reaches a despair beyond the succor of man.

While Edgar's subconscious mind in hypnosis was still orthodox enough to envision the soul as a creation of God which contains a minute particle of Him at its core, the reader will have clearly seen by now how adamantly he maintains that all mortal sorrow comes from the soul's own misuse of the free will given it by its Maker.

In short, God can neither denounce, sit in judgment condemn, mete out punishment, be cajoled by lip-service, nor award special dispensations to a favored few. He relinquished all these privileges when he gave every soul freedom of action, choice and decision. Now, He can only wait in patience and genuine compassion for the souls to decide how soon they will use their free will to return to Him, once they have conceded that He makes a better Creator than they do.

The reader may argue that as a theory it may all

be very fine, and even acceptable to the subconscious, but it leaves conscious man in the uncomfortable position of having nowhere to pass the buck, and the ego depends for its self-preservation on the illusion that it is more sinned against than sinning.

If we return to that first session with Lammers in 1923 we should by now find it easier to trace the fundamental logic underlying Edgar's philosophy.

LAMMERS: What is the soul of a body?"

CAYCE: "That which the Maker gave to every individual in the beginning, and which is now seeking the house—or place—of the Maker."

LAMMERS: "Does the soul ever die?"

CAYCE: "It may be banished from the Maker. That is not death."

LAMMERS: "How does the soul become banished from its Maker?"

CAYCE: "To work out its own salvation—as you would term the word—the individual banishes itself."

LAMMERS: "What is meant by the personality?"

CAYCE: "The personality is that which is known on this physical plane as the conscious. When the subconscious controls, (e.g. under hypnosis) the personality is removed from the individual and lies above the physical body. This may be seen here (in my own case).

"Hence the disturbing of these conditions would bring distress to the other portions of the individual."

This point was dramatically illustrated some years later when Hugh Lynn Cayce, Edgar's son, was conducting a public session. One of the men present scribbled a note and handed it to Hugh Lynn across the sleeping body of his father, who instantly broke off speaking and relapsed into a cataleptic silence, which thoroughly disconcerted his son. The situation was without precedent and he had no means of resolving it. Some hours later, Edgar suddenly jackknifed from his recumbent position and catapulted himself to his feet at the base of the couch. This was done with unbelievable rapidity, more akin to the speeded-up action of a film than anything in reality, and while Hugh Lynn was still grappling with his own amazement, his father asked in a perfectly natural voice for something to eat. He had an intense hunger and thirst.

In a subsequent Reading he explained that his "personality"—evicted from his physical body by the self-hynotic process—had levitated about a foot and a half above his physical body. And when the gentleman had handed the note to Hugh Lynn, he had thrust his fist through the astral equivalent of Edgar's rib cage. The impact was the equivalent of a kick from a horse.

This ability of the body to separate itself into at least three separate levels of electric vibration—much as the atomic scientists have divided the atom into separate energies, all different but all coexistent—can only manifest itself in cases as unique as Edgar Cayce's. He could move from plane to plane of consciousness with the ease of a man switching from AM to FM and then to TV on the same console.

The basic logic is perfectly simple: the least effective part of any unit—spiritual, human or mechanical—is its most temporary component. In the human makeup, the physical body, the "temporary shelter" of the eternal soul, is the most expendable.

The lizard who can always grow another tail (should he happen to lose one through no fault of his own) is not likely to attach exaggerated importance to that particular section of his anatomy. He is secure in the knowledge that, while he can grow another tail, the tail cannot grow another him.

Unfortunately, the human ego is incapable of such lucid reasoning. To mix the metaphor and take it to

127

its logical conclusion—in the human psyche, the tail stubbornly insists on wagging the dog. Therein lies the beginning and the end of all human misery. This is what led Sartre's existentialists to blind themselves with inexact science, and avante-garde clerics, seeking to escape still further from all spiritual responsibility, to create Instant Religion out of God-is-deadism.

THE SAME LAW GOVERNS ALL PLANETS

"The unbalancing of the truth brings normal results to both the physical and soul matter," Edgar Cayce told Lammers. "Each individual must lead his own life, whether in this sphere or in the other planes."

We might take this to mean that the eternal laws of cause and effect, to which every soul is personally answerable, work on all the other planets in our system exactly as they do on earth, even though this is the only planet where physical life as we know it exists.

The components of the other planets may be as diversified as the atoms in nuclear physics. Their *genera* may range from one-dimensional to the cube root of x-dimensional. But each makes its proper contribution to the eventual evolution of the soul.

"All insufficient matter is cast into Saturn," said Cayce at this time, implying that the planet in question may operate as a kind of oven, slow-baking the accumulated drosses out of those souls who have fallen so far behind the others that immediate return to the earth would cause hardship for all concerned—the bigots of history, possibly, from Herod down through the Roman and Byzantine tyrants to this century's dictators and their schizoid worshippers.

Thus, if Edgar Cayce is correct in suggesting that

each planetary environment tempers the wind to the shorn lamb, the soul's reception here must always be dictated by the condition in which it arrives, whether from another planet in the solar system, or from the various astral confines of our own.

LAMMERS: "Where does the soul come from, and how does it enter the physical body?"

CAYCE: "It is already there. As the body of the human, when born, breathes the first breath of life, so it becomes a living soul, provided it has reached that development where the soul may rightly enter and find a lodging place."

LAMMERS: "Is it possible for this body, Edgar Cayce, in this state, to communicate with anyone who has passed into the spirit world?"

CAYCE: "The spirits of all that have passed from the physical plane remain about that plane until their development carries them onward, or until they are returned for their further development here. While they remain within the plane of communication of this sphere, any may be communicated with. There are thousands about us here at present. . . ."

THE PLANETARY INFLUENCES

LAMMERS: "Give the names of the principal planets, and their influence on the lives of people."

CAYCE: "Mercury, Mars, Jupiter, Venus, Saturn, Neptune, Uranus, Septimus."

LAMMERS: "Are any of the planets, other than the earth, inhabited by human beings or animal life of any kind?"

CAYCE: "No."

LAMMERS: "Give the description of the planet nearest the earth at the present time, and its effect upon the people."

CAYCE: "That planet now fast approaching the earth, under whose influence the earth minds trend for the next few years, as time is known here, will be Mars, which will be only thirty-five million miles away from the earth in 1924.

"The influence will be felt as this recedes from the earth and those who have sojourned on Mars will express, in their lives upon the earth, the troublesome times that will arise. This will only be tempered by those who will be coming from Jupiter, Venus and Uranus, those strong ennobling forces tempered by love and strength."

THE ASTROLOGICAL INFLUENCES

LAMMERS: "Please define astrology."

CAYCE: "The inclinations of man are ruled by the planet under which he is born, for the destiny of man lies within the sphere or scope of the planets.

"In the beginning, our own planet, the Earth, was set in motion. With the planning of other planets began the destiny of all created matter.

"The strongest force affecting the destiny of man is the Sun first, then the closer planets to the earth, or those that are coming to ascension at the time of the birth of the individual.

"Just as the tides are ruled by the Moon in its path about the earth, just so is the higher creation ruled by its actions in conjunction with the planets about the earth.

"BUT LET IT BE UNDERSTOOD HERE: NO ACTION OF ANY PLANET OR THE PHASES OF THE SUN, THE MOON, OR ANY OF THE HEAVENLY BODIES, SURPASSES THE RULE OF MAN'S OWN WILL POWER: the power given by the Creator to man in the beginning, when he became a living soul with the power of choosing for himself. . . .

"In the sphere of many of the planets within the same solar system, we find souls again and again and again return, from one to another, until they are prepared to meet the everlasting creator of our Universe, of which our system is only a very small part. (But) only upon the earth plane, at present, do we find men in flesh and blood. Upon others do we find those of His own making in the preparation of His own development."

THE SOUL'S IMMUNITY TO DEATH

How does the world of the living appear to the soul who is temporarily free of an earth-body? The simplest frame of reference might be to compare the weight and density of an astronaut on the ground with his weight and density in orbit.

There is definite evidence that an astronaut, once he is beyond the pull of earth's gravity, attached to the capsule only by a thin nylon cord, experiences moments of exhilaration, euphoria, a disassociation with the earth below him, and a desire to remain suspended in space.

Suppose we argue, then, that the difference between the soul freed by death, and the same soul encased in a living body is only a difference of density and vibration, no more complex than the difference between the astronaut floating in space and the same astronaut securely strapped to his controls before takeoff. Before takeoff he has little or no freedom of action; in outer space he has more than he needs, but in essence he is still the same man.

Once you feel you can accept this comparison, it may be easier for you to go back to the Creation and

131

imagine the souls as they first became aware of themselves.

The earth was still cooling from its fiery birth; the division of land and water had followed. Then came the emergence of animal life from its amoeboid origins. The only solid matter the souls had ever known was now manifesting itself on the earth proper. In other words, only the earth itself conformed to the laws of density and gravity as we know them now.

Hovering above the earth, the souls had been following this evolutionary progress with fascination, and now, with the division of animal life into male and female species, their curiosity tempted them to digress from their own evolutionary path and assume mortal shape instead. At this time, remember, their bodies were still of rarified spiritual texture. In terms of the astronaut, they were "weightless."

Cayce constantly employs the term "thought-forms" when dealing with their condition at this stage of their development. A thought-form is exactly what its name suggests: a form created by concentrated thought, yet lacking the solidity of mundane matter. On all mental levels other than the conscious mind, "thoughts are things," and thus a thought-form, once it is created, is as real and tangible as the mind which created it.

It can only manifest itself to the conscious mind as a vision or a hallucination. Injudicious doses of lysergic acid break down the protecting barrier and submit the user to direct contact with thought-forms, usually his own; though he is equally vulnerable to the thought-forms of others. When these outside contacts are evil, his encounters with them can have a disastrous after-effect on his own sanity.

When a competent hypnotist tells a susceptible subject in a trance that he is holding an orange in his empty hand, and the subject obediently begins to eat it, he is, to all intents and purposes, eating a real orange. He has created a thought-form of it at that level of his subconscious where thought *is* matter.

Cayce explained that the uncorrupted soul could enter and withdraw from denser matter at will, being able to "push out of itself" and adapt to the conditions which had already taken shape in its thought "much in the way and manner that the present-day amoeba sustains itself in the waters of a stagnant bay or lake."

Because it had never been God's intent that the souls should ever manifest themselves on this earth in human bodies, there was as yet no division of the souls into male and female. Therefore, the animals' means of reproduction was inaccessible to them. Their only alternative was to "occupy" the animal bodies, much as a hermit crab might occupy the empty shell of another species, except that in this case, the shells were already occupied!

Thus two entirely alien forms of life were attempting to share a common physical heritage. The hazards were obvious. Nevertheless, a few of the bolder souls employed their free will to intrude into this denser vibration of animal matter.

The wiser and more prudent souls hesitated, and it was well that they did.

Those souls which now found themselves entrapped in their flesh prisons were unable to extricate themselves. The alien matter of the material world acted like the cogs of an implacable machine. It engorged the souls and swept them along with it. They became hopelessly entangled in the procreative processes. And onto the earth came an anguished hybrid, neither human nor animal—a half-man, half-beast—unable to conform to or escape from the laws of animal evolution.

"We find these sons of the Creative Forces," says Cayce, "looking upon those changed forms, the Daughters of Men. And there crept in those pollutions; or rather, they polluted themselves with those mixtures. This brought contempt, hatred, bloodshed, and those impulses which build for self-desire, without respect for another's freedom."

The souls who had remained free were unable to come to the rescue. They could only look on, helpless and bewildered.

It was this that caused God to create a perfect physical mold, or flesh body, into which the "rescue-souls" could incarnate with safety. Symbolized in Genesis as the creation of Adam, man appeared in his present form at five different places on the earth, and each of the five newly created groups was ethnically distinct from the others.

The souls who now incarnated through these pure channels are referred to by Cayce as the *Sons of God* to distinguish them from the souls trapped in animal matter. These he called the Sons of Man.

The Bible's admonitions to "keep the race pure" have their origins in this first appearance of uncontaminated souls on the earth. To them, the hybrid souls with their animal deformities were in the Hindu sense "untouchable."

The Sons of God, in their five separate race categories of white, black, brown, red, and yellow pigmentation, built up their separate civilizations on continents now destroyed or altered beyond recognition by the subsequent earth-changes. The Atlantic ocean now covers the submerged continent of Atlantis (cradle of the red race), just as the Pacific covers the sunken continent of Lemuria (cradle of the black race).

Because so few questions were put to Edgar Cayce concerning it, the Readings record very little of Lemuria. But Atlantis (200,000 B.C. to 10,700 B.C.) is generously documented. Indeed, according to the Readings, it is fair to assume that it was the cradle of our present civilization.

This vast soul-group was both the most aggressive and the most resourceful the world was ever to know.

For the most part, the Atlantean influence is still as headstrong as ever it was. This influence applies particularly to those soul-groups who chose *not* to reincarnate at a steady rate of progress. At their zenith, the Atlanteans commanded the powers of ESP and telepathy, harnessed electricity, mastered the mechanical propulsion of air and sea vessels, established short wave communications, induced longevity and performed advanced surgery, using as their source of energy the Tuaoi Stone of "Terrible Crystal" their own forerunner of the maser or laser ray. It was the misuse of this same source of energy which destroyed them.

They were a peripatetic, restless expression of human life, perpetually striving to meddle with, alter and improve the laws of Nature. They attained to a fantastic height of power, and then proceeded to abuse it.

From their spiritual beginnings as a civilization that only recognized the One God, they eventually rejected Him for a totalitarian god of brute force, which is the same as saying that they worshipped their own vices instead.

They reduced the backward hybrid souls, or mutants, to slavery, subjecting them to every degradation and abuse.

They remained perfectly aware of the laws of karma, but made the error of assuming that their accumulating debts could easily be paid off at any given time in the future. Here they reckoned without one factor—that the path of evolution might suddenly

135

veer in its course and return them to meet their debts in bodies shorn of all their Atlantean prescience and might.

This is exactly what befell them. When man's senses were reduced to the minimal five he possesses today, the Atlantean miscreant found himself as impotent as the hermit crab bereft of its shell.

The karmic debts that were to be so easily paid off in a life or two were suddenly magnified into infinity. Instead of two lives, some of their offenses against God now demanded thousands of lives of restitution.

Rather than shoulder such eternal burdens, they chose spiritual bankruptcy. The vast accumulation of debt remains, however, and still has to be paid.

Early in this century, Edgar Cayce began to prophesy the return of both types of Atlanteans in vast numbers. He warned that for every advance of science and material emancipation the Sons of the One God might bring with them, the Sons of Man could also bring corruption and chaos.

"Atlantean souls are extremists; they know no middle ground," Cayce stated uncompromisingly, adding that Atlanteans of every genre were to be found among the leaders of all the nations involved in the two World Wars. So, as a rough standard of comparison, we can set Roosevelt and Churchill at one end of the scale and Hitler and Stalin at the other. In like manner we can contrast Pope John XXIII with Mao.

The advances which civilization has made from barbarism to practicable democracy leave the impenitent type of Atlantean unmoved, except when his stupefaction that "his world is not as it was" reaches a psychotic level. Then he stuffs himself with LSD, or climbs into a college bell tower and shoots the "usurpers who have altered the earth." At a cannier level of self-preservation, he is the scofflaw whose cynicism undermines his society. You will find him behind the corrupt politician, the rabble rouser, the lunatic fringe dedicated to religious and racial discrimination, and the gougers of the sick, fat buck, who are reducing the popular cultures to semi-literate trash.

"As we have indicated, the Atlanteans were those who had reached an advancement and had been entrusted with divine activities in the earth, but forget the One God in Whom all live and have their being. Thus they brought about that which destroyed the body, though not the soul. There are numbers, great numbers, of Atlanteans in the earth in the present."

Against the extremist Atlanteans who still worship lust, violence and death, are aligned the sober forces of their tempered, experienced fellow-souls, who have gained a sane perspective from their many and varied reincarnations down through history—"those strong ennobling forces tempered by love and strength." With these marches the Christ. With these may lie our descendants' only means of averting another cataclysm akin to the annihilation of Atlantis.

This concept is thrown into sharp focus when the Life Reading for a very young child warns its parents that in its Atlantean life, it had worshipped the One God.

The usurpers of power at the time of the third and final inundation, however, were the Sons of Belial, whose god of evil was destined to survive the Deluge in the corrupted form of the Biblical idol Baal. The child had suffered persecution at the hands of these same Sons of Belial, "as it will again here in the present. Let the Entity be warned to guard against all those who seek for self."

"Granting that reincarnation is a fact," Edgar Cayce said elsewhere, "and that souls once occupied such an environ as Atlantis, and that these are now entering the earth's sphere—if they made such alterations in the earth's affairs in their day as to bring destruction on themselves—can there be any wonder that they might make such like changes in the affairs of peoples and individuals today?"

This same warning is reiterated in another Reading: "Beware lest material or vain things bring thee forgetfulness of Who is thy Redeemer, and whence cometh the Voice which is deep within! For what is needed most in the world today? That the Sons of Belial be warned that those who are, and have been, unfaithful to the One God must meet themselves in the things which come to pass."

In one of his Readings for a child, Edgar urged the parents to direct his interests towards the technical side of "radio, television and the like" because his experience in electrical communications stemmed from a life in Atlantis in which he had been an expert in the use of sound-waves "and the manner in which light was used as a means of communication. And Morse's dots and dashes were already 'old-hat' to the Entity in that experience."

Elsewhere he counsels a young man with an Atlantean "memory-bank" to choose electronics as a career because "none of the modern conveniences are a mystery to the Entity, even though he may not understand them as yet. For the Entity has always expected to see these again!"

The advanced technology which Atlantis's scientists brought back to this century with them has controlled disease, conquered the skies and split the atom, but it has also bequeathed us the H-Bomb—that selfsame exploitation of nuclear energy which destroyed its original creators and buried their arrogant ramparts deep in the mud of the ocean floor.

Why has this totalitarian cross section of a once mighty race learned nothing from its blunders? Because it refused to keep abreast of the world's spiritual progress by reincarnating in its proper soul-cycles. But surely its greatest lack is its ignorance of Christ. Its last memory of life on earth predates, by nearly two hundred centuries, the Redemption brought to the soul of man by the Master. It is hardly likely, then, that our articles of faith are imposing enough to command the comprehension or respect of such atavists. Remembering nothing of Christ, they have no cause to abandon their ancient belief in the brute survival of the fittest. They would be as eager today to enslave the more backward nations as they enslaved the backward humanoids of their own time ... those selfsame "things" or "monstrosities" whom the Sons of the One God led out of Atlantean bondage into prehistoric Egypt, where the surgeon-priests in the temples of healing eradicated the physical evidence of their animal antecedents and "made them men.

"This is the purpose of the Entity in the earth," Cayce taught, "to be a living example of that which He gave: 'Come unto Me, all that are weak and heavy-laden; Take My cross upon you and learn of Me.' These are thy purposes in the earth. And these thou wilt manifest beautifully—or again bring to miserable failure, as thou didst in Atlantis, and as many another soul is doing in this particular era."

The final Armageddon, said Cayce, will not be fought on the earth. It will be fought between the souls leaving the earth and the souls endeavoring to return to it—the souls returning to the God they once deserted, and the lost souls who hope to reject Him into eternity, by holding fast, at all costs, to this failing planet.

In terms of orthodox dogma it will be a war fought between the dead, not between the living.

But Edgar Cayce makes no more differentiation between the dead and the living than he does between the caterpillar, the cocoon and the butterfly. Thus the souls involved in the final Armageddon will be the same souls they always were from the Beginning. Nothing will have changed except the plane of consciousness they occupy. They will only have moved from the confines of matter to the eternal plane of their origin.

CHAPTER NINE

EDGAR CAYCE'S OWN CREDO

In 1941 Edgar Cayce had occasion to give a Reading to two members of the Association for Research and Enlightenment, in which he commended them for resolving their own karmic differences in their dedication to the work of the Association. They had successfully buried the hatchet and worked side by side to such a harmonious extent that the writer Thomas Sugrue was able to assemble his biography of Edgar, *There is a River,* from the material they had patiently indexed from the Readings.

There had been mutual forgiveness by both members, the Reading explained, "for each has met himself well. Remember the injunction given by Him: 'When thou art converted, strengthen thy brothers.' Do not depart from the awareness that He, the Master, Jesus, will walk with thee—if ye desire to walk with Him."

In the distant past, these two members had been enemies in more than one life—not so much because their ideals conflicted, but because they were serving the same ideals at cross-purposes. Rather than hating one another, they had been jealous of each other's glory; the war between their egos had taken precedence over their service to their fellow men and delayed their spiritual progress down the centuries.

It is in this same Reading that Edgar gave voice to his own intense concern for the unenlightened soul in the period immediately following physical death. If the soul has lived in ignorance of the unbroken flow of life from one plane of consciousness to the next, he may "pass over without understanding until the opportunity for understanding is seemingly past."

He voiced a hope that the A.R.E. would succeed in building the truth "in each phase of an individual's experience while he is on earth—in books, in pamphlets, in lectures, by conversation—in such a manner that knowledge, and the wisdom to apply it, be made available to all who choose to seek it."

His total reliance on the power of Christ to preserve and enlighten the human soul underlies his every thought. In 1932, when he was asked to give the strongest reason against reincarnation, he answered: "That a law of cause and effect should exist here in material things. Yet the strongest argument against reincarnation is also the strongest argument for it, as in any principle reduced to its essence. For the law is set, and it happens—even though a soul might will itself never to reincarnate, but would prefer to suffer and suffer and suffer—for both Heaven and Hell are built by the soul.

"But does a soul have to crucify the flesh, even as He, when it discovers that it must work out its own salvation in the material world by entering and reentering until it achieves that soul-consciousness which would make it a companion with the Creator? . . .

"Rather is the law of forgiveness made available in thine experience through the Son who would stand in thy stead."

Cayce never professed to be a man of letters in his waking state, but what he did write is impressively lucid and never obscured by pretension. The proof is evident in this talk he gave to the A.R.E. in 1933, where he explained his own attitude to his psychic power in words that would be hard for another pen to better.

"As to the validity of the information which comes through me when I sleep—this is the question, naturally, that occurs to everyone. Personally, I feel that its validity depends largely upon how much faith and confidence lie within the one who seeks this source of information.

"In regard to this same source of information, even though I have been doing this work for thirty-one years, I know very little about it. Whatever I might say would be largely a matter of conjecture. I can make no claims whatsoever to great knowledge, for I also am only groping.

"But then, we all learn by experience, do we not? We come to have faith and understanding only by taking one step at a time. Most of us don't have the experience of getting religion all at once, like the man who got it halfway between the bottom of the well and the top, when he was blown out by an explosion of dynamite! Most of us need to arrive at our conclusions by weighing the evidence along with something that answers from deep within our inner selves.

"As a matter of fact, there would seem to be not just one, but several sources of information tapped when I am in this sleeping state.

"One source, apparently, is the record made by an individual in all of its experiences through what we call time. The sum total of the experiences of that soul is written, so to speak, in the subconscious of that individual as well as in what is known as the Akashic Records. Anyone may read these records, if

143

he can attune himself rightly. Apparently, I am one of the few people who may lay aside the personality sufficiently to allow the soul to make this attunement to the universal source of knowledge. I say this, however, not in a boastful way; in fact, I don't claim to possess any power that any other person doesn't possess. I sincerely believe that there isn't any person, anywhere, who doesn't have the same ability I have. I'm certain that all human beings have much greater powers than they are ever aware of—provided they are willing to pay the price of detachment from self-interest which is required to develop those powers or abilities. Would you be willing, even once a year, to put aside your own personality—to pass entirely away from it?

"Many people ask me how I prevent undesirable influences from entering into the work I do. In order to answer that question, let me tell an experience I had when I was a child. When I was between eleven and twelve years of age, I had read the Bible three times. Now I have read it fifty-six times. No doubt some people have read it more times than that. But I have tried to read it once for each year of my life.

"Well, as a child, I prayed that I might be able to do something for other people—to aid them in understanding themselves, and especially to aid children in their ills. One day I had a vision which convinced me that my prayer had been heard and would be answered.

"So I believe that my prayer is still being answered. And as I go into the unconscious condition, I do so with that faith. I also believe that the source of information will be from the Universal, if the connection is not made to waver by the desires of the person seeking the Reading.

"Now, some people think that the information coming through me is given by some departed person-

144

ality who wishes to communicate—some benevolent spirit or guide from the other side. This may sometimes be true, but in general I am not a 'medium' in that sense of the term. If the person who seeks a Reading, however, comes seeking that kind of contact and information, I believe he receives that kind.

"For instance, if that person's desire is very intense to have a communication from Grandpa, Uncle, or some great soul, then the contact is directed that way, and such becomes the source.

"Do not think I am discrediting those who seek in such a way. If you're willing to receive what Uncle Joe has to say, that is what you get. If you're willing to depend upon a more Universal Source, then that is what you get.

" 'What ye ask, ye shall receive' is like a two-edged sword. It cuts both ways."

Two years earlier, he had told the A.R.E. audience he was addressing: "Now who is to be the judge as to what is the proper way and manner in which to conduct research into the mysteries of life? We are able to judge only by their fruits, only by the results people obtain, when they delve into these phenomena of life.

"I am constantly asked by people who have just come to know me: "Are you a spiritualist? How did you ever become interested in psychic phenomena? Are you a medium? Are you this, that, or the other?"

"It has always been my desire to be able to answer for the faith that lies within. It seems to me that if one cannot answer for that faith that one professes to live by, then such a one is not at his best. For we live by faith, day by day. If we don't know what we believe or why we believe it, we are indeed getting far afield from that which the Source of Life would have us be.

"What is Life? What is this phenomenon of life?

Where and how do the various phenomena manifest themselves?

"We have a physical body; we have a mental body; we have a spiritual body, or soul. Now each of these has its own attributes. Just as the physical body has its divisions—all dependent one upon the other, and some more dependent than the rest—so the mind has its own source of activity that manifests in various ways through the individual body.

"The soul also has its attributes, and its various ways of gaining, maintaining or manifesting itself among men. The psychic force is a manifestation of the soul mind.

"Let us go back into sacred history. Do you know where the first lines were drawn concerning psychic phenomena? Where the first line was drawn as to what a psychic phenomenon is—the division as to what is real, and what is not?

"It was when Moses was sent down into Egypt to deliver the Chosen People, and he was told to take the rod he had in his hand and—with Aaron, his brother—to go before Pharaoh. God, through him, would show mighty wonders to the people. Then Moses went before Pharaoh and cast his rod down, and it turned into a serpent. The magicians cast their rods down, and they turned to serpents, too. But Aaron's rod or serpent ate up all the rest of them!

"Then there began what were called the plagues in Egypt. In one, Aaron stretched out his rod over the waters and they turned to blood. The magicians stretched out their rods, too, and the water turned to blood for them. Next came the plague of frogs, and the magicians could do this also, with their enchantments. Then came the plague of lice, when the rod smote the dust of the earth; and this plague was the first instance of blood being drawn from the body. The magicians attempted to do the same thing but nothing happened. They turned to Pharaoh and said: 'The finger of God is in this thing!' (Ex. 8:18, 19)

"At this point, we can draw a dividing line between enchantments and the things of God. When we know, when we are convinced, when we see by the results, that the finger of God is indeed in what is taking place, then we can know whether the phenomenon we are seeing and experiencing is of divine origin or otherwise!

"How may it be otherwise? Well, we say all force, all power, comes from one source. With that I agree; but when there is a misapplication of this Force of Life itself, the phenomenon does not fail to occur—even though misdirected. Just as we see people born among us who are mentally deficient, physically disabled. Apparently such afflictions have nothing whatever to do with the individuals. (I say apparently). Yet the phenomenon of life moves on, just the same. At some point there has been a misdirection or a guiding-away from the purposes of the All-Powerful. Yet it moves on just the same.

"Possibly there wasn't a greater parable than the one about the wheat and the tares growing up together. The tares were not to be rooted up at once, else the wheat would be destroyed also. But the time would come when the wheat would be gathered and put into the granary, and the tares gathered to be burned.

"If the soul is in a proper accord with the Source of life, may not the phenomena be directed by the same One that directed Aaron, rather than that which directed the magicians in their activity? In the plagues, there was a point at which the magicians failed. So if psychic phenomena come from some source other than the one Divine Source, they, too, must reach a point where they fail.

"The Master was in accord with the One Source of

147

all Good. I think many others also were, at various times, when they presented themselves as a living sacrifice, holy and acceptable unto Him. Therefore, it must be possible for any of us to be in accord with the One Divine Source of all information, if we will but pay the price.

"Often I have fallen far short in presenting myself as a living sacrifice for whatever source might manifest through me. In that sense, I suppose I may be called a medium. But I hope I may be, rather, a channel through which blessings may come to many, rather than a medium through which any force might manifest. For if it is of God, it must be good. Or, if it is good, it must come from the All-Good, or God. This good, I trust, is the type of psychic phenomena manifesting through me."

This is a serene manifesto of perfect faith, couched in a simplicity that lends it beauty. And Cayce's personal love and trust in the Christ is, if possible, even more intimate in its total dedication when he spoke to the same group in 1934.

"In John 14: 1-3, Jesus said: 'Let not your heart be troubled; ye believe in God, believe also in Me . . . And if I go and prepare a place for you, I will come again, and receive you unto myself; that where I am, there ye may be also.'

"When we look into the history of the world as we know it today, how often has a great religious leader or prophet arisen? Plato said that our cycle of entering is about every thousand years. Judging from history itself, the period of time between each religious teacher who has come into the earth varies from six hundred and twenty-five years to twelve hundred.

"Do you ask: 'Is that how often you say Christ has come?'

"No, I don't say that. I don't know how many times He has come. However, if we will consider the following passages of Scripture for a few moments, an interesting idea may be formulated: 'In the beginning was the Word, and the Word was with God, and the Word was God. The same was in the beginning with God. All things were made by Him; and without Him was not anything made that was made . . . And the Word was made flesh, and dwelt among us. . . . He was in the world, and the world was made by Him, and the world knew Him not.' (John 1: 1-14.)

"Many people tell us that this is speaking of spiritual things. You must answer this for yourself. But if the Word was made flesh and dwelt among men, how can we be sure that this is not speaking materially, too?

"In talking with those who should have been and were the judges of Israel at the time, the Master said: 'Your father Abraham rejoiced to see my day, and he saw it, and was glad.' Then said the Jews unto Him, 'Thou art not yet fifty years old, and hast thou seen Abraham?' Jesus said unto them, 'Verily, verily, I say unto you, before Abraham was, I am.' (John 8:37-44.)

"Did Jesus mean that in a spiritual sense or a literal sense—or both? What do you think? I don't know. But what we have been told psychically is this—take it for what it is worth and apply it in your own experience.

"Now turn to the fourteenth Chapter of Genesis and read where Abraham is paid tribute by a certain royal priest, Melchizedek, who brought forth bread and wine. 'For this Melchizedek, King of Salem, priest of the most high God, who met Abraham returning from the slaughter of the Kings, and blessed him. . . . Without father, without mother, without descent, having neither beginning of days, nor end of life, but made like unto the Son of God; abideth a priest continually.' (Hebrews 7.)

"Was this the Master; this Melchizedek? I don't know. Read it yourself. Maybe I'm wrong in thinking it was the Master; the man we know later as Jesus.

"Consider now the book of Joshua. Who directed Joshua when he became the leader of Israel? Who walked out to lead Joshua, after he crossed the Jordan? The Bible says that the Son of Man came out to lead the armies of the Lord. And after Joshua's experience in meeting this man of God, all the children of Israel were afraid of him. (Joshua 5:13-15.)

"From the above references, let us draw a few conclusions, and supplement them with psychic information. The Spirit of the Christ manifested in the earth many times before the coming of Jesus at times it manifested through one like Melchizedek, and at other times it manifested as a spiritual influence through some teacher upholding the worship of the One God.

"What has this conclusion to do with the second coming? Well, in the light of the above, there ceases to be a second coming! Also, by considering the conditions that made His appearance possible at various times—or, if you prefer, the one time as Jesus—we can deduce certain facts about the return of the Master.

"How did He happen to come as Jesus of Nazareth? There had not been a revelation to man, of which we have any record, for over four hundred years. Then did darkness and dissipation on the part of man bring Christ into the World? If so, it's a reversal of the natural law Like begets Like. The laws of God are not reversed at any time, and never will we find them so. They are immutable and hold true throughout any kingdom we may find in the earth.

"Then what brought about the coming of Jesus? A people who were sincere seekers—a little group founded to make themselves channels whereby this great thing could come to pass. Who were these people? They were the most hated of all those mentioned in profane history, and are scarcely mentioned in the Bible, the Essenes, the hated ones, the lowest of the Jews. . . .

"These Essenes, then, were consecrating their lives to make possible a meeting place for God and man, that Jesus the Christ might come into the world. Thus there was a *preparation;* and if we will prepare a meeting place—in our heart, our home, our group, our church—then we too can have the Christ come to us again, and He will come as He is. His spirit is here always. It will abide with us always. . . .

"We all believe that He descended into Hell and taught those there. We read it in the Bible and we say it is true. But we don't really believe it. If we did, we would never find fault with any soul in the world— never! For if we believe that He went into Hell and taught the people there, how could we find fault with out next-door neighbor because his chickens got into our garden, or because he doesn't believe exactly as we do?

"He, for our sakes, became flesh. How many times? Answer for yourself. How soon will he come again? When we live the life He has laid out for us, we are making it possible for Him, the Lord and Master of this world, to return.

" 'I will not leave you comfortless, but I will come again, and receive you unto myself; that where I am, there ye may be also.' "

Thus in his waking hours Cayce the man reveals himself as a tolerant and sincere churchgoer of orthodox antecedents, with no desire whatever to push his personal beliefs down other people's throats . . . or for them to push their beliefs down his throat. Nevertheless, it would be difficult to proceed beyond this point to a fully-balanced explanation of

151

reincarnation as he saw it, unless we understood his insistence that Christ was a Divinity manifesting himself through a highly-developed human soul named Jesus. Furthermore, that same Divinity had had to manifest Itself several times on earth before It was able to prepare a human body of sufficiently advanced spirituality to sustain It in Its ultimate task of salvation.

The reader may be assured that no Reading exists in which Edgar Cayce infers that sections of the Bible had been re-edited with malice aforethought. When he was asked if such might be so, he replied that the spirit of the Bible was still whole, and that its power lay in its spiritual strength, and was not dependent on its literal context. In short, it was still God's assurance to the human race that He would never abandon it.

On the other hand Cayce did not, in permissive sleep, deny that many sections had lost their original clarity in the course of their translations from Hebrew to Byzantine Greek, to classic Latin, and then to Jacobean English. A thorough study of the Readings centering round the Palestinian period at the time of Christ reveals that they gave the Essenes far greater credit for preserving the true wisdom of the ancient scriptures than the established Hebrew Church, which was, in effect, passing through the type of period which Pope Pius XII has defined as "heresy of action."

When Christ preached in the synagogues, he introduced nothing new or unfamiliar into his sermons, but, more devastatingly, he revived those sections of the old teachings which had either fallen into convenient disrepute, or been reinterpreted to suit the political exigencies of the Sanhedrin.

It is pertinent to inject here that the Dead Sea Scrolls, even in these cautious early stages of their deciphering, have established that much of Christ's teaching is present in the same form, indeed often in the same words, in the Essene scriptures which were in existence at least a hundred years before His birth.

This proves that He was in basic accord with the tenets of the Essenes, although in His own lifetime they were in such militant conflict with orthodox Judaism that no reference to them was permitted in the Hebrew Scriptures.

Unfortunately the sect possessed its fair share of firebrands and hotheads who believed that the ends justified the means, even to the extent of guerilla attacks on the caravans of the Sadducees and the Pharisees. This group obviously found itself in conflict with Christ's exhortation to resist all forms of violence, and even the two or three Essenes among His disciples forgot themselves often enough to provoke incidents which achieved no better purpose than to heighten the antagonism of His enemies.

At this time, Jerusalem was occupied by the Romans very much as France in our century was occupied by the Nazis—but the Essenes were a sect which had for so long been underground that they were virtually unaffected by the superimposition of Roman persecution over the existing persecution of the Sanhedrin. Nevertheless, the sect met eventual annihilation at the hands of the Roman army, at the instigation of the Sanhedrin, the same governing body which had instigated the crucifixion of Christ.

To some, what the Dead Sea Scrolls are slowly establishing is that the Essene beliefs were rooted firmly in the laws of reincarnation.

Furthermore, they were the only sect which correctly prophesied the coming of Christ. Just as the books of the Apocrypha and Revelation were obscured in symbolism to preserve the truth they contained, the Essene prophecy is worded in the past instead of the future tense, and in it Christ is called by variations of the Good Man, the Messiah, and the Son of Light, never by His real name; and the Sanhedrin is referred to as the Wicked Priest. In every other respect it is an exact foretelling of the events which came to pass a century later.

Cayce states categorically that the Essenes, being the only sect that was prepared for Christ's appearance on earth, not only aided in the birth in the manger and the flight to Egypt, but taught Jesus in his childhood. Many of these teachers were recognized by Cayce in the present:

"Then, the Entity was brought up in the tenets or school of thought that attempted to be a reconstruction of the former sect established by Elijah in Mount Carmel. . . .

"Because of the divisions that had arisen among the peoples into sects such as the Pharisees, the Sadduccees, and their kind, there has arisen the Essenes, who cherished not merely the traditions which had come down by word of mouth, but had kept records of all supernatural experiences—whether in dreams, visions, or voices—that had been felt throughout the experiences of this peculiar people. . . .

"These pertained, then, to what you would call today astrological forecasts, as well as all those records pertaining to the coming of the Messiah. These had been part of the records in Carmel given by Elijah, who was the forerunner, who was the cousin, who was (John) the Baptist. . . .

"Hence the group we refer to here as the Essenes was the outgrowth of the teachings by Melchizedek, as propagated by Elijah and Elisha and Samuel. The movement was not an Egyptian one, though it was adopted by the Egyptians in an earlier period and made a part of the whole movement. They took Jews and Gentiles alike as members . . . preserving themselves in direct line of choice as channels through which might come He of the new or the divine origin. . . .

"The Essenes were to aid in the early teaching of the life of the child Jesus, as well as of John. For John was more the Essene than Jesus. For Jesus held rather to the spirit of the law, and John to the letter of same."

Throughout the detailed and exhaustive references to Jesus in the Readings, one is constantly struck by the urgent reality of the prose. Edgar Cayce always refers to Him as an immediate, living Force, never further from man than his own elbow.

CHRIST THE MESSENGER; JESUS THE MAN

If, as Edgar Cayce reasons, Christ manifesting Himself through the body of Jesus was completing His own soul development in the earth, it brings conviction to His assurance to His disciples that they were capable of doing all the things that He had done. This was obviously impossible if they were to remain as spiritually imperfect as they were at that time. It presupposed that they would return many times before they could attain to His enlightenment.

Otherwise, we would have to believe that Christ was demanding of His followers an almost super-human exercise in blind faith. He was offering a hit-or-miss, one-chance-only hope of survival . . . only if we sin no more, may we enter heaven. Is it so easy to conceive of Him as such an impractical perfectionist? All His other teachings are, in every sense, practical and realistic.

Cayce found it much more consistent that He defined the eventual redemption of the soul as a slow, patient retracing of the footsteps, rather than "instantaneous apotheosis." In this context, reincarnation appeals to the self-doubter not to despair as he watches his nimbler brothers apparently outstrip him. It teaches him that his free will can work for his best interests just as easily as it can work against them. He is shown the way—after that, it is up to him. He must take up his own bed and walk, not be transported bodily to an ersatz Heaven by an all-too-mortal Redeemer.

He is taught that if an innocent man, having suffered injustice at the hands of a powerful enemy, grimly takes a "just" revenge, he will gratuituously handcuff himself to that same enemy, and both of them will be compelled to return together and re-enact the whole dreary, negative conflict until they develop enough common sense to bury their hatchets and call it quits. The more advanced soul of the two is bound to delay his own spiritual progress, for he has forced himself to proceed at the speed of the less developed soul he has harmed.

If, on the other hand, he is smart enough to "turn the other cheek" rather than attempt a futile retaliation, he frees himself of all further involvement with his enemy. The onus is then on his enemy, who must return alone, in his own time to repair whatever damage he left in his own wake.

WHO IS WITHOUT SIN

Why did Christ make no social distinction between Pharisees and whores, publicans and weighty scholars? Surely because their outer trappings were temporary and transient, and He was concerned solely with the ultimate welfare of the soul within, as it struggled onward through its slow and painful self-exile.

156

What else is Christ saying, when He bids us love our neighbor, except: "Don't be such a fool as to hate him, and involve yourself with the dead weight of another gratuitous enemy!"

Christ was never more tolerant and merciful than in His treatment of the woman taken in adultery. Indeed, He was putting the law of love into practice in a way that very few of the churches bearing His name seem anxious to emulate. And yet all He was saying, in effect, was: "As ye judge, so shall ye be likewise judged." He was warning the woman's tormentors that in their subsequent lives they ran the danger of being caught in *flagrante delicto,* if only to teach them to shun persecution and hypocrisy, the two drabbest cancers of the soul.

His parable of the Prodigal Son restores God to the perspective that had been distorted in the Old Testament, when the scattered nomad tribes used the avenging Jehovah as a big stick to keep their spear-happy warriors from exterminating first their fellow tribesmen and eventually themselves.

Thus the parable of the Prodigal Son only takes on its true universality when God becomes the forgiving Father, and the Son becomes the lost and wandering soul on earth, afraid to return to its Father in metaphorical rags.

The Chalcedonian Decree of 451 A.D., which split Christ into two separate natures, human and divine, is confirmed by Edgar Cayce's answer to the same question:

"Christ is not a man! Jesus was the man! Christ was the Messenger! . . . Christ in all ages! Jesus only in one!"

Unless He was preparing himself to return to His disciples in a body akin to the purified shape they themselves would one day assume when they, too, eventually returned to their Father, why did Christ, on the cross, withdraw from his mortal form long enough for Jesus to call to Him in bewilderment: "Eli, Eli, why hast thou forsaken me?" It is utterly contrary to all His own teachings that Christ should have given way to inexplicable misgivings at the eleventh hour, and called those words to God. It would have served no better purpose than to harrow and demoralize those of his followers whose faith in Him, till then, had been absolute.

Surely Christ's logical purpose in submitting to the crucifixion was to show His followers not only the ease with which the earthly ties of flesh can be discarded, but the total unimportance of the body after it ceases to house the soul.

It is in this regard that Edgar Cayce puts forward a theory which occurs nowhere in dogmatic controversies, yet seems the most lucid of them all.

(Here it must be borne in mind that he refers to the living body as the body material, and the body after death as the body physical.)

"Just as an Entity, finding itself in one of those various realms abounding in the solar system, takes on, not an earthly form, but a pattern conforming to the elements of that particular planet or space, the Prince of Peace came into the earth in human form for the completing of His own development. He overcame the flesh and all temptation. So He became the first to overcome death in the body, enabling Him to so illuminate and revivify that body as to take it up again, even when those fluids of the body had been drained away by the nail holes in His hands and by the spear piercing His side. . . ."

Cayce insisted that Christ had already begun to assume His own immortal form when Mary Magdalene saw Him in the company of the two angels:

"As indicated in the spoken word to Mary in the Garden: 'Touch me not, for I have not yet ascended

158

to my Father' . . . the body as seen by the normal, or material, eye of Mary was such that it could not be handled until there had been the conscious union with the Source of all Power. . . ."

Cayce then proceeded to analyze verses nineteen through twenty-nine, from the twentieth chapter of St. John:

"Just as indicated in the manner in which the body-physical (the spirit body) entered the upper room with the doors closed, not by being part of the wood through which the body passed, but by forming itself from the ether waves that were already within the room, because of a meeting prepared by faith . . . 'Children, have ye anything here to eat?' indicated to the disciples present that this was not transmutation but a regeneration of the atoms and cells of the body. . . ."

It may at first glance seem curious to place such vital emphasis on this concept of Christ, which on the face of it would have little bearing on the attitude of the western churches to reincarnation. But it is over this very issue that the grimmest controversies in the church's early history raged, and one of its many consequences was the rejection of reincarnation from western faith.

Before we proceed to trace this from its source to its effect on present-day orthodoxy—which in its turn served to increase the burdens under which Edgar Cayce labored—we submit the parallel views on the same Biblical passages as they are put forward by the famous English cleric, Leslie D. Weatherhead, M.A., Ph.D., Hon. D.D., Minister of the City Temple, London, and Honorary Chaplain to Her Majesty's Forces:

"Students of the resurrection never seem to me to have paid enough attention to the meticulous details about the grave-clothes which the fourth Gospel gives. This narrative—unlike some parts of the Gospel —seems to me to be based on the account of an eye-witness.

"It is made clear that the grave-clothes, covering the body up to the armpits, had collapsed as if the body had evaporated. We are told that the turban wound round his head stood on its edge, as if the head also had evaporated. If the student will turn to the twentieth chapter of the fourth Gospel and read the first twenty verses, he will realize that it was the way the grave-clothes were lying that convinced Peter and John that Christ had disposed of his physical body in a way which we do not understand, but which suggest words like 'evaporation,' or 'evanescence.'"

It would seem a far cry from the testimony of a lone clairvoyant to an established pillar of orthodox English Methodism, but almost nowhere else does so much corroboration exist for Edgar Cayce's religious philosophy than in the clear and forthright prose of Dr. Weatherhead.

THE CHRISTIANITY OF CONSTANTINE

In his *Psychology, Religion and Healing*, Abingdon Press, Dr. Weatherhead states: "The conversion of the Roman Emperor Constantine to Christianity in 325 A.D. was a very doubtful gain to the cause of Christ. He may have seen a cross in the sky surrounded by the words In Hoc Signo Vinces, but he produced a Christianity that dispensed with the Cross, and might as well have used a cushion as its symbol.

"The Name above every name had once been written on the pale foreheads of the young knights of Christ who had either died for Him in the hundreds, or ridden forth to declare to a sneering and indifferent world the good news of the Gospel. That was over now. But it was a disaster that Constantine was 'converted.' . . .

"Christianity became, in fact, a polite veneer without power or beauty. All the Court darlings were Christians now. The spineless sycophants who giggled out their fatuous days in the luxury of the Roman court, and the sleek, shrewd parasites who battened on its energy and power, were 'converted' overnight. . . .

"Paganism remained, but now it was labelled Christianity as it is today. The religion of Christ has never recovered either, except for brief periods of revival, and without a nucleus of real saints it could not have survived."

VOLTAIRE

If we now turn to the genius of Voltaire (1694–1778), one of history's greatest scholars as well as a founding father of democracy, we find that these excerpts from his *Philosophical Dictionary* anticipated Dr. Weatherhead's arguments with admirable acerbity.

"By the end of the first century there were some thirty gospels, each belonging to a different society, and thirty sects of Christians had sprung up in Asia Minor, Syria, Alexandria and even in Rome," says Voltaire. "Two or three antiquaries, either mercenaries or fanatics, enshrined the barbarous and effeminate Constantine, and treated the just and wise Emperor Julian as a miscreant. Subsequent chroniclers, copying from them, repeated both their flattery and their calumny. Finally, the age of sound criticism

161

arrived, and after fourteen hundred years, enlightened men reviewed the judgment of the ignorant.

"Constantine was revealed as an opportunist who scoffed at God and men. Here is how he reasoned: 'Baptism purifies everything. I can therefore kill my wife, my son, and all my relatives. After that I can be baptized, and I shall go to Heaven.' And he acted accordingly. But he was a Christian, and he was canonized...."

THE COUNCIL OF NICAEA, 325 A.D.

One school of dogma claims that reincarnation was condemned at the Council of Nicaea, in which case Voltaire's own analysis of its purpose deserves inclusion here:

"Alexandras, Bishop of Alexander, saw fit to preach that God was necessarily individual and indivisible—that He was a monad (a single unit) in the strictest sense of the word, and that this monad was triune (three in one). Alexandras's monad outraged the priest Arius, who published a denunciation of the theory. Alexandras quickly summoned a small council of his adherents and excommunicated his priest....

"The Emperor Constantine was villain enough to send the venerable bishop Osius with conciliatory letters to both warring factions, and when Osius met with justified rejection, the Council of Nicaea was convened.

"The question to be considered was: Is Jesus the Word? If He is the Word, did He emanate from God in time, or before time? If He emanated from God, is He co-eternal and consubstantial with Him: or is He of a similar substance? Is He made or begotten? And how is it that, if He has exactly the same nature and essence as the Father and the Son,

He cannot do the same things as these two people who are himself?

"This I cannot understand. No one has ever understood it. And that is why so many people have been butchered.

"The final decision of the Council of Nicaea was that the Son was as old as the Father and consubstantial with the Father . . . and war raged throughout the Roman Empire. This civil war gave rise to others, and down through the centuries to this day, internecine persecution has continued. . . .

"(Yet) Jesus taught no metaphysical dogmas. He wrote no theological treatises. He did not say: 'I am consubstantial; I have two wills and two natures with only one person.' To the Cordeliers and the Jacobins, who were to appear twelve hundred years after Him, He left the delicate and difficult task of deciding whether His mother was conceived in original sin.

"The Socinians, or Unitarians, call the acceptance of this doctrine of original sin the 'original sin' of Christianity. It is an outrage against God, they say. . . .

"The Socinians place much emphasis on the faith of the first 'heretics' who died for the apocryphal gospels, (and) refuse therefore to consider our four divine Gospels as anything other than clandestine works.

"To dare to say that He created all the successive generations of mankind only to subject them to external punishment, under the pretext that their earliest ancestor ate of a particular fruit, is to accuse Him of the most absurd barbarity.

"This sacrilegious imputation is even more inexcusable among Christians, since there is no mention of original sin, either in the Pentateuch or in the Gospels, whether apocryphal, or canonical, or in any of the writers called the First Fathers of the Church.

163

"Souls were either created from all eternity (with the result that they are infinitely older than Adam's sin, and have no connection with it), or they are formed at the time of conception. In which case God must create, in each instance, a new spirit which He must then render eternally miserable, or God is Himself the soul of mankind, with the result that He is damned along with His system. . . ."

And finally Voltaire gets to the heart of the matter thus: "None of the early Fathers of the Church cited a single passage from the four gospels as we accept them today.

"(They) not only failed to quote from the gospels, but they even adhered to several passages now found only in the apocryphal gospels rejected by the canon.

"Since many false gospels were at first thought to be true, those which today constitute the foundation of our own faith may also have been forged."

ORIGEN

This brings us logically to the teachings of Origen (185 A.D.–254 A.D.), around which all the controversy was now to center.

Origen's teachings were vital to the preservation of the original gospels. His pen had been as prolific as Voltaire's, but according to the *Encyclopedia Britannica* then ten books of "Stromata," his most provocative work, have disappeared leaving almost no trace. This is of paramount significance, in that Origen occupied himself here in correlating the established Christian teachings with the "Christian" dogmas of Plato, Aristotle, Numenius and Corrutus. He devoted his life to the preservation of the original gospels.

"It was not so much the relation between faith and

knowledge that gave offense, but rather isolated propositions such as his doctrine of the preexistence of souls. . . . Origen was able to explain the actual sinfulness of all men by the theological hypothesis of preexistence and the premundane fall of each soul."

Origen states in his own *Contra Celsum:* "Is it not more in conformity with reason that every soul, for certain mysterious reasons, (I speak now according to the opinion of Pythagoras and Plato, and Empedocles, whom Celsus frequently names), is introduced into a body according to its desserts and former actions? Is it not rational that souls who have used their bodies to do the utmost possible good should have a right to bodies endowed with qualities superior to the bodies of others?

"The soul, which is immaterial and invisible in its nature, exists in no material place without having a body suited to the nature of that place. Accordingly, it at one time puts off one body—which was necessary before, but which is no longer adequate in its changed state—and it exchanges it for a second."

And in his *De Principiis:* "Every soul . . . comes into this world strengthened by the victories or weakened by the defeats of its previous life. Its place in this world as a vessel appointed to honor or dishonor, is determined by its previous merits or demerits. Its work in this world determines its place in the world which is to follow this."

PYTHAGORAS AND PLATO

Exactly how did the "pagan" philosophies of Pythagoras and Plato (who both subscribed to reincarnation) complement the beliefs of the Early Christian Fathers?

The views of Pythagoras (582–507 B.C.) exist only

in his biographies by Diogenes Laertius and Iamblichus, but the former quotes him as asserting that "he had received the memory of all his soul's transmigrations as a gift from Mercury, along with the gift of recollecting what his own soul, and the souls of others, had experienced between death and rebirth."

From Plato (427–347 B.C.), we can obtain direct context: "Soul is older than body. Souls are continuously born over again into this life.

"The soul of the true philosopher abstains as much as possible from pleasures and desires, griefs and fears . . . for in consequence of its forming the same opinions as the body, and delighting in the same things, it can never pass into Hades in a pure state, but must ever depart polluted by the body, and so quickly falls into another body, and consequently is deprived of all association with that which is divine and pure and uniform.

"Know that if you become worse, you will go to the worse souls, and if better, to the better souls; and in every succession of life and death, you will do and suffer what like must fitly suffer at the hands of like."

It should also be established here that St. Jerome (340–400 A.D.) once impulsively hailed Origen as "the greatest teacher of the Church since the Apostles." This is hardly plausible if the New Testament was then as ambiguous in its references to reincarnation as it is now. Surely for Origen to have held pride of place among the Early Church Fathers for nearly four centuries, his tenets must have been based solidly on what at that time were accepted as the true gospels.

St. Clement of Alexandria (150–220), in his *Exhortation to the Pagans* is also clearly influenced by Plato: "We were in being long before the foundation of the world; we existed in the eye of God, for it is our destiny to live in Him. We are the reasonable creatures of the Divine Word. Therefore, we have existed from the beginning, for in the beginning was the Word. . . . Not for the first time does He show pity on us in our wanderings. He pitied us from the very beginning."

To St. Jerome's and St. Augustine's views on Plato must be added those of St. Gregory (257–332), who affirmed that "it is absolutely necessary that the soul should be healed and purified, and if this does not take place during its life on earth, it must be accomplished in future lives."

St. Augustine (354–430), held Plato in such veneration that he writes in his *Contra Academicos:* "The message of Plato, the purest and the most luminous of all philosophy, has at last scattered the darkness of error, and now shines forth mainly in Plotinus, a Platonist so like his master that one would think they lived together, or rather—since so long a period of time separates them—that Plato was born again in Plotinus."

To come full circle, Plotinus (205–270) was a fellow-disciple with Origen under Ammonius, who founded the famous Alexandrian School of Neoplatonism in Egypt in 193 A.D.

Plotinus, in *The Descent of the Soul,* is perhaps the most articulate and expressive: "Thus the soul, though of divine origin, having proceeded from the regions on high, becomes merged in the dark receptacle of the body, and being naturally a postdiluvial god, it descends hither through a certain voluntary inclination, for the sake of power and of adorning inferior concerns. . . .

"Yet our souls are able alternately to rise from hence, carrying back with them an experience of what they have known and suffered in their fallen state, from whence they will learn how blessed it is

167

to abide in the intelligible world, and by a comparison of contraries, will more plainly perceive the excellence of a superior state.

"For the experience of evil produces a clearer knowledge of good . . . the whole of our soul does not enter in the body, but something belonging to it always abides in the intelligible world, which is something different from this sensible world, and that which abides in this world of sense does not permit us to perceive that which the supreme part of the soul contemplates."

Here we have the testimony of four Saints of the early Church. They cannot *all* have had bats in the belfry, nor would they have embraced beliefs that were hostile to the contemporary tenets of their own church. The fact that they repeatedly adhere to the "Christian" dogmas of Plato indicates their conviction that Christ had included those same dogmas in His own philosophy.

Exactly when did these original versions of the Gospels undergo such drastic reinterpretation? In all the research material that is reasonably available, there is not one source which can supply a clear-cut, substantiated answer, and only the *Catholic Encyclopedia* even hints at one.

CHAPTER TEN

DOES THE BIBLE CONDEMN
REINCARNATION?

"I can read reincarnation into the Bible—and you can read it right out again!" Edgar Cayce once said with his usual dry humor. Though he had read the Bible once for every year of his life, his first reaction in Dayton was to read it straight through again to find where it actively condemned the theory of reincarnation. Nowhere did it do so. Nowhere did it endorse reincarnation per se, either; but in Proverbs 8:22-31 he found this strangely moving reference to Creation: "The Lord possessed me in beginning of His way, before His works of old.

"I was set up from everlasting, from the beginning, or ever the earth was.

"When there were no depths, I was brought forth . . . when He prepared the Heavens, I was there. When he appointed the foundations of the earth, then was I by Him, as one brought up with Him. And I was daily His delight, rejoicing always before him, rejoicing in the habitable part of His earth. And my delights were with the Sons of Man."

Are we beholden to take this as the abstract imagery of an obscure poet? Or can we ask who "I" was? Obviously not a mortal creature with a life-span of three score years and ten; no matter how obscurely he was expressing his poetry. If we credit "I" with being a human soul, speaking of its own origin from its subconscious memory; every line makes logical sense. Its nostalgic yearning for the uncorrupted joy of its beginnings, its longing for its rejected God, these epitomize perfectly the weary soul's disenchantment with the arid cycle of its materialistic lives on earth, having cut itself off from its loving Father as the Prodigal Son had done.

This is not the dour "predestination and original sin" of Calvin's luckless humanoid, damned before he draws his first breath, potential fuel for the eternal fires even before he quits the womb. It is not the despair of the damned; it is only the cry of the lost sheep.

With this as our model, how should we interpret this line from the Wisdom of Solomon 8:19-20: "Now I was a good child by nature, and a good soul fell to my lot. Nay, rather, being good, I came into a body undefiled."

The King James Version, with curious circumlocution, takes this liberty: "For I was a witty child, and had a good spirit. Yea, rather, being good, I came into a body undefiled," making a non sequitur of the whole passage. But in both versions, who is the arbiter of what is good and what is bad? Clearly the soul itself, using its own standard of previous conduct as its gauge, in that it makes no claim to having been designated 'good' by standards other than its own. And surely it could have no means of knowing what 'good' was, unless it was equally familiar with its opposite?

That souls had been both good and bad at various stages of their manifestation on earth is again implied in Romans 9:11-14: "For the children being not yet born; neither having done any good nor evil. . . . it was said unto (Rebecca), 'The elder shall serve the younger. As it is written: Jacob have I loved, but Esau have I hated.' What shall we say, then? Is there unrighteousness with God? God forbid."

If there is "no unrighteousness" with God, why is God showing a most ungodly bias by loving Jacob for no reason, and hating Esau for no reason? What opportunity would either of them have found, before their creation, to chose such divergent natures? If they had come directly from their Maker to Rebecca's womb, where else could Esau have committed his crimes, except in Heaven? If he did, why wasn't he cast out with the rest of the fallen angels and deposited directly into hell? It would seem far more likely that he learned to sin on earth, in a mortal body, and his return as the servant of his younger brother was an act of restitution.

"Even from everlasting to everlasting, Thou art God," says the Ninetieth Psalm. "Thou turnest Man to destruction, and sayest 'Return, ye Children of Men.' . . . Thou carriest them away as with a flood; they are asleep; in the morning they are like grass that groweth up." Here we have the ambiguity of the word "turnest" to contend with; the lyrist having combined the tribal Jehovah with the Creator. A fairer reading would surely be, "Thou failest to turn man from his destruction." Even so, the concept of Heaven in those days was an eternal state of static perfection. "If 'Return, ye Children of Men' meant 'return to Heaven' (the only alternative being the Fiery Pit), then the three transpositions from flood to sleep to growing grass are not only bad imagery but disjunct. Even if we accept the 'flood' literally to mean death by drowning (the Flood, after all, was fairly recent history), and the 'sleep' to symbolize an interim

171

period between death and resurrection in Heaven, 'the grass that groweth up in the morning' is still a peculiar symbol for a Heavenly life where all is perfect and nothing alters. The earthly seasons, on the other hand, do alter. The grass grows up with every spring to die again with every winter; and the reincarnating soul follows an identical cycle."

The theme suggests itself again in Job 1:20-21: "Then Job arose and rent his mantle, and shaved his head, and fell down upon the ground and worshipped. And said: 'Naked came I out of my mother's womb, and naked shall I return thither!' "

Obviously if Job is referring literally to the same mother, the old gentleman has lost his marbles. But if we accept the fact that Job was not an historical character but a symbol for the soul, the parable is exhorting man never to despair when all seems lost, and the symbolism of the womb at once becomes self-evident. The soul cannot possibly embark on its next life on earth without first 'returning naked to the womb.'

And what is the reward of the soul, once it completes its earth cycles and can return like the Prodigal Son to the Father it rejected when it chose to glorify itself instead? "Him that overcometh," Revelation 3:12, "will I make a pillar in the Temple of the Lord, and he shall go no more out."

In Malachi 4:5, we come to perhaps the most persuasive example of all, for Elijah and Elias are only variations in spelling; both refer to the same prophet. "Behold," says Malachi in the fifth century B.C., "I will send you Elijah the prophet before the coming of the great and dreadful day of the Lord."

Five hundred years later, according to Matthew 16:13, "When Jesus came into the coasts of Caesarea Phillipi, he asked His disciples, saying, 'Whom do men say that I, the Son of Man, am?'

"And they said, 'Some say that Thou art John the Baptist, some Elias; and others, Jeremias, or one of the Prophets.'" This is continued in Chapter 17, Verse 10. "And His disciples asked Him, saying, 'Why then say the scribes that Elias must first come?'

"And Jesus answered and said unto them, 'Elias truly shall first come and restore all things. But I say unto you that Elias is come already, and they knew him not, but have done unto him whatsoever they listed. Likewise shall also the Son of Man suffer of them.' Then the disciples understood that He spake unto them of John the Baptist."

What logical thought-process induced the disciples to draw such a conclusion so promptly, unless Jesus had made them thoroughly familiar with the laws of reincarnation? John the Baptist had been beheaded by Herod in their own lifetime, and Elias was five hundred years dead.

The idea that the soul could reincarnate must have been equally familiar to Herod, for in Luke 9:7-8: "Herod the tetrarch heard of all that was done by (Jesus); and he was perplexed, because it was said of some that John was risen from the dead; and of some that Elias had appeared; and of others that one of the old prophets was risen again. And Herod said, "John have I beheaded, but who is this of whom I hear such things?' And he desired to see Him."

The curiosity of an orthodox monarch would hardly have been aroused by irresponsible talk. He would have cleared his court of the superstitious idiots who entertained such fancies and attached no further importance to Jesus.

And in the light of the above, what are we to make of this passage from John 9:1-3? "And as Jesus passed by, he saw a man which was blind from birth. And his disciples asked him, saying, 'Master, who did sin, this man or his parents, that he was born blind?' Jesus answered, 'Neither has this man sinned nor his parents. He was born blind that the works of God should be made manifest in him.' "

If reincarnation was a totally rejected theory, surely Jesus's answer would have been a reproach for such an idiotic question. Obviously a newborn babe is incapable of any kind of sin: if sin had been the cause of the blindness, then the question would have been phrased quite differently: "Master, is this the sins of the father's visited on the child, or are the parents innocent of sin?" Jesus was in all things merciful. Even when he "cursed" the fig tree (in the non-melodramatic sense of blighting it). He had obviously divined that it was rooted in subsoil sufficiently contaminated to poison its fruit. He would never have painted such a forbidding picture of his Father as to suggest He inflicted a defenseless child with blindness merely to "manifest His works in him." But if the soul inhabiting the man had voluntarily elected to be blind, to advance itself more swiftly in patience and understanding, then the works of God would most assuredly be made manifest in him.

Interpreted from the point of view of karma, Jesus's restraining doctrine of "as ye sow, so shall ye reap" makes perfect good sense. Shorn of its basic link to reincarnation, it dwindles to fatuous banality. Very few people are fortunate enough to reap what they sow in the same lifetime.

The disciples were simple fishermen and men of the soil, and Jesus's tone changes when he debates with an educated man of the world like Nicodemus.

The following passages from John 3:3-14 are usually interpreted as applying only to the pros and cons of baptism; but the text does not imply it, and it is hard to conceive of Jesus descending to a straw-splitting quibble over the niceties of proper church usage with a mature scholar of Sanhedrin law. The passages make a great deal more sense if we assume that Jesus is chiding a man who should know better than to give His symbolic words a purely literal interpretation.

He hardly seems to be prescribing secular baptism as the solution for Nicodemus's confusion, when He makes the unequivocal statement: 'Verily, verily, I say unto thee; except a man be born again he cannot see the kingdom of God.' Nicodemus said unto Him: 'How can a man be born when he is old? Can he enter a second time into his mother's womb and be born?' Jesus answered: 'Verily, verily, I say unto thee, except a man be born of water and of the Spirit, he cannot enter unto the kingdom of God. That which is born of flesh is flesh, and that which is born of the Spirit is spirit. Marvel not that I say unto thee, "Ye must be born again." The wind bloweth where it listeth, and thou hearest the sound thereof but canst not tell whence it cometh or wither it goeth. So (it is with) everyone that is born of the Spirit.'

"Nicodemus answered and said unto Him, 'How can these things be?' Jesus answered and said unto him, 'Art thou a master of Israel and knowest not these things? .... If I have told thee of earthly things and ye believe not, how shall you believe if I tell you of heavenly things? And no man has ascended up to Heaven, but that he came down from Heaven; even the Son of Man which is in Heaven.' "

If we proceed to Chapter 8, Verse 34 of the same gospel; Jesus, arguing with the orthodox Jews in the temple, speaks with such slight concern for their prejudices that he is stoned for his pains. If we are still to assume that the argument centers only around the right way and the wrong way to conduct a baptism, it is hard to understand why He wasted His patience and energy over such a trivial issue. If the issue is their rejection of reincarnation, however, His following words and the resultant fury they arouse fall into a very logical perspective. " 'Verily, verily, I say unto you, whosoever committeth sin is the servant of sin. And the servant abideth not in the house (the flesh) for ever; but the Son abideth ever. If the Son, therefore, shall make you free, ye shall be free indeed. . . . I speak that which I have seen with my Father; (but) ye do that which you have seen with your father.'

"They answered and said unto Him, 'Abraham is our father!' Jesus said unto them, 'If ye were Abraham's children, ye would do the works of Abraham. But now ye seek to kill me . . . this did not Abraham. . . . Your father Abraham rejoiced to see my day; and he saw it and was glad.'

"Then the Jews said to him, 'Thou are not yet fifty years old, and hast thou seen Abraham?'

"Jesus said unto them, 'Verily, verily, I say unto you; before Abraham was, I am.'"

Why are these allusions to reincarnation in the Bible so isolated and fragmentary? Is it possible that the few that do exist were accidentally overlooked during a systematic expurgation of the original Greek and Hebrew texts?

For the moment it is sufficient to establish that Edgar Cayce satisfied himself that an acceptance of reincarnation in no way went against Holy Writ: it did, in fact, add teeth to many of its arguments.

Without question, it supplies force and logic to the warning: "He that killeth with the sword must be killed with the sword, and he that leadeth into captivity, must be led into captivity." (Revelation 13:10.)

"As thou has done, it shall be done unto thee; thy reward shall return unto thine own head." (Obadiah 1:15.)

But perhaps the most impressive warning of all, directed, it would seem, to those who might be tempted to tamper with the true meaning of the Gospels to further their own aggrandizement, is given by Jesus in Luke 11:52: "Woe unto you, lawyers! for ye have taken away the key of knowledge; ye entered not in yourselves, and them that were entering in, ye hindered."

In the newly discovered Coptic Gospel according to St. Thomas* this is directed squarely at the church: "The Pharisees and the Scribes have received the keys of Knowledge, and have hidden them. They did not enter, and they did not let those who wished."

* Harper and Row (N.Y. 1959), p. 25.

CHAPTER ELEVEN

WHY ISN'T REINCARNATION IN THE BIBLE? THE HIDDEN HISTORY OF REINCARNATION

Our orthodox versions of the Old and New Testaments date no further back than the sixth century, when the Byzantine Emperor Justinian summoned the Fifth Ecumenical Congress of Constantinople in 553 A.D. to condemn the Platonically inspired writings of Origen.*

Contrary to the belief of our contemporary Churches, this was not an unsecular Congress. The Pope was forbidden to attend, and his denunciation of it was flouted. It was instigated by the same substratum of moronic barbarians who had 'converted' to Christianity under Constantine.

If the reader should find it singular that this Congress is given so much attention in the following pages, it is because the events which led up to the Fifth Congress represent practically the only surviving evidence as to why reincarnation disappeared from the Bible.

The Byzantine Emperor Justinian (483–565), as a fatherless youth, was brought up in austere obscurity

* See appendix A.

by his mother and his uncle, the "peasant" Emperor Justin, while they rigidly groomed him to inherit the throne of Constantinople. The severity of his upbringing was responsible for an arid, erratic streak in him. He early developed an intellectual passion for law that is hardly commensurate with normal adolescence, and though he considered himself essentially a "good" man, he was easily swayed by flattery and his judgment of his fellow men remained superficial and immature.

Only in his intuitive grasp of military strategy was he consistent. His youthful General, Belisarius, successfully subdued the Ostrogoths in Italy and the Vandals in Africa, thus restoring the foundering Roman Empire to a modicum of its former power.

Byzantine architecture flowered under Justinian, and he revised Roman law to the extent that it subsequently became the basis for all western civil law.

On the face of it, he should have risen to the heights of a Charlemagne. That he did not was due in part to his temperament—an incompatible mixture of dedicated zealotry and infirmity of purpose—and in part to his deterioration to the rank of pawn in a ruthless woman's bid for self-deification.

Theodora (508–547), the commoner who became Justinian's Empress, wielded sufficient authority over contemporary records to suppress most of the evidence of her dubious background, and her only contemporary biographer, Procopius, so bitterly detested her that his *Secret History* is rejected in as many academic quarters as it is accepted in others.

It is generally agreed that Theodora was the daughter of a bear-feeder in the amphitheatre in Constantinople, and made her debut as a child actress at a time when that profession ranked with the world's oldest. Of this, too, she rapidly became an accomplished member, and her insatiable ambition made capital of the obstacles that confronted her.

Theodora's strategy was always to create a condition of organized confusion in which every man eventually found himself in conflict with his neighbor, enabling her to divide and conquer at her leisure. Once she had become Justinian's mistress, she set her stakes even higher. She determined to become his Empress, and though Justinian's mother opposed her with all the power at her command, Justinian proved to be too emotionally unstable to resist such a blitzkrieg.

Where his knowledge of his fellow men was faulty and erratic, Theodora's was expert and innately predatory. Where he vacillated, she was as inflexible as iron. Although the law forbade men above senatorial rank to marry actresses, the law was conveniently abolished by Justinian on the death of his mother, and Theodora took her place beside him on the throne.

There is nothing historically unique about an unworldly monarch reduced to thralldom by a ruthless courtesan, but few courtesans in history possessed Theodora's diabolism.

Witness the *Encyclopedia Britannica:* Officials took an oath of allegiance to her as well as to the Emperor. The city was full of her spies, who reported to her everything said against herself or the administration. She surrounded herself with ceremonious pomp, and required all who approached to abase themselves in a manner new even to that half-Oriental court.

"According to Procopius, she had before her marriage become the mother of a son, who when grown up, returned from Arabia, revealed himself to her, and forthwith disappeared for ever."

In very short order she became a tyrant in the grand manner of the more psychotic Caesars.

Her favorites catapulted to power and her enemies died in such numbers that eventually the public rose up against the royal couple. Confronted by the Nika insurrections of 532, Justinian, terrified and demoralized, would have fled before it, but the indomitable Theodora preferred death to obscurity. She made him sweat it out, and the riots were finally subdued.

After that, Justinian was no more impressive than a glove-puppet on her strong right hand, and she was free to concentrate her energies on the most formidable of her foes, the Church of Rome.

Theodora saw the Christian Church as her equivalent of the Great Pyramid—an eternal monument to her ego—and to ensure its permanency she set about the total reconstitution of its credenda, which were far too sublime for her purposes. That she actually succeeded was due to the fact that the Vatican had barely had time to recover from its subjugation by Theodoric the Ostrogoth before it found itself under the over-solicitous "police protection" of Belisarius's army of occupation.

Her first and most influential teacher, Eutyches, a devotee of the Eastern Church, first emerged when Theodora was the mistress of Hecebolus, the governor of Pentapolis in North Africa. When Hecebolus eventually threw her out of the city, Theodora and Eutyches gravitated first to Alexandria and then to Constantinople, she as an ascending power in the lists of profane love, and he as the doyen of a series of Monophysite religious schools.

THE MONOPHYSITE DOCTRINE

The Monophysite doctrine is, as it were, the villain of the piece.

It was this sect that was later to discredit all allusion to reincarnation in the early gospels, and split the church into two warring factions.

It must be remembered that not only had an unending series of conflicting schisms plagued the solidarity of the Christian Church from about 300 A.D. onward, but it also faced active resistance and sturdy competition from the pagan religions it had not yet superseded, many of which were not only gayer and more escapist, they even threw in the odd saturnalia.

Now the Monophysites added to the confusion by contending that Jesus's physical body was wholly divine, and had never at any time combined divine and human attributes. (It seemed to cause them no embarrassment that Jesus himself had declared that there was a spark of the divine in every human soul. They adhered militantly to their conviction that the mere act of donning the outer trappings of a mortal body would have defiled Jesus's true origin.)

Unfortunately, under the influence of Eutyches, Theodora became a convert to this controversial Monophysite dogma. Its principal claim to her affections was its total rejection of those teachings of Origen which had so profoundly influenced the early Church Fathers. Origen not only believed in metempsychosis, but argued that Christ the Logos, or Word, inhabited the human body of Jesus, thus sanctifying it.

It is fair to assume that Theodora conscripted two of her most devoted deacons, Virgilius and Anthimus, on the suggestion if not the insistence of Eutyches, to this viewpoint.

It is difficult, today, when one wades through these laborious arguments between the Eastern and Western branches of the Church over the divinity of Christ, to realize the manic antagonism they aroused in both camps. The Monophysites continued to provoke strife and discord until the year 451, when a specially summoned Church Council, loyal to Origen's teachings, split Christ into two separate natures, human and divine.

THE CHALCEDONIAN DECREE, 451 A.D.

The well-intentioned decision known as the Chalcedonian Decree, while protecting the teachings of Origen, became, in effect, the launching pad for all the black mischief that followed.

Indeed the split between the Monophysites and the Vatican eventually reached such violent proportions that "one of Justinian's first public acts was to make the Patriarch of Constantinople declare his full adhesion to the creed of Chalcedon." (*Encyclopedia Britannica*)

This constitutes solid evidence that, prior to Theodora's arrival on the scene, Justinian was in complete sympathy with the Origenist leanings of the Church of Rome; yet in 543, at Theodora's urging, he permitted a local synod to discredit and condemn the writings of Origen.

Very much as the hero of Orwell's *1984* "purified" the public files of the newspapers by rewriting political history and eliminating all reference to previous "Big Brothers," Theodora now pursued a campaign designed to obliterate all and any passages in the Bible which might reduce to absurdity her hopes of instant apotheosis upon departing this life.

ANTHIMUS

Theodora's first move in her grand strategy was to subdue and unify the various feuding factions of the Eastern Church until it was utterly under her domination. In open defiance of Vatican protocol, she appointed her lackey Anthimus as Patriarch of Constantinople.

Now Anthimus is a minor figure in the overall picture, but he was equipped for great mischief at this moment. Theodora had appointed him for the express purpose of revoking the Chalcedonian Decree. Justinian's role, as usual, was to plead ignorance of the whole affair and play Pilate.

At once she ran afoul of Pope Agapetus.

POPE AGAPETUS

This dignified old worthy traveled from Rome to Constantinople in bleak February weather, and when he discovered the full enormity of Theodora's intent, he became the only prelate ever to denounce her in Constantine's presence.

"With eager longing," he informed the outraged Justinian, "have I come to gaze on the most Christian Emperor Justinian. In his place I find a Diocletian,* whose threats, however, terrify me not!"

This unexpected rap on the royal nose pulled Justinian up short, and "being fully convinced that Anthimus was unsound in faith, he made no exception to the Pope's exercising the plenitude of his powers in deposing and suspending the intruder Anthimus and, for the first time in the history of the Church, personally consecrating his legally elected successor, Mennas." (*Catholic Encyclopedia*, p. 203)

Unfortunately for the spiritual destiny of Europe, the saintly and incorruptible Agapetus died in the same year of 536; but he leaves a nobler and more honorable record behind him than any of the other participants in this sorry charade.

---

* One of the tyrant Cæsars.

His expedient demise followed his triumph so swiftly that one can only assume that Theodora was instrumental in speeding him to a happier world.

With Agapetus dead, Mennas was easily brought to heel, and accommodatingly condemned the entire Diocese of Origenism in the Emperor's name.

From this point on, Justinian obediently sanctioned all Theodora's further purges of Origenism.

POPE SILVERIUS

It seems relevant at this point to illustrate from a completely independent source, the *Vita Silveri* (Gesta Pont. Rom. I. 146), just how malevolent Theodora's self-deification had become:

"Because the Empress was grieving for the Patriarch Anthimus, the most holy Pope Agapetus having deposed him on the grounds of heresy and replaced him with Virgilius, she sent this letter to (Agapetus's successor) Pope Silverius at Rome: 'Make no delay in coming to us, or without fail recall Anthimus to his own place!'

"And when blessed Silverius had read this, he groaned and said: 'I know very well that this affair has brought an end to my life,' but replied by letter to the Empress: 'Mistress Augusta, I shall never consent to do such a thing as to reinstate a man who is a heretic and who has been condemned in his own wickedness.'

"Then the Empress, in a fury, sent orders to the patrician (General) Belisarius by the deacon Virgilius: 'Seek out some grounds of complaint against the Pope Silverius that will remove him from the office of Bishop, or at least send him quickly to us. You have there the Archdeacon Virgilius, our most beloved deputy, who has promised us to recall the patriarch Anthimus.'

"The patrician Belisarius undertook the commission, and under urgent orders, certain false witnesses issued forth and actually made the statement that they had discovered the Pope Silverius sending messages to the King of the Goths. Upon hearing this, Belisarius refused belief, knowing that these reports were motivated by envy. But when many more persisted in this same accusation, he became afraid.

"Therefore he caused the blessed Pope Silverius to come to him in the Pincian Palace, and he stationed all the clergy at the first and second entrances, and when Silverius and Virgilius had come alone into the salon, the patrician Antonina was reclining on a couch, and her husband Belisarius was seated at her feet. Antonina said at once: 'Tell me, Master Silverius, Pope; what have we done to you and the Romans, that you wish to betray us into the hands of the Goths?'

"And even while she was speaking these words, there entered John, the regional sub-deacon of the first ward, who lifted the blessed Pope Silverius' collar from his neck and led him into a chamber. There he unfrocked him, put on him monk's garb, and spirited him away.

"And Virgilius took him under his personal protection, as it were, and sent him into exile in Pontus, where he sustained him with the bread of tribulation and water of necessity. And he weakened and died and became a confessor."

Theodora now stood revealed in her true colors, and her next move was her most ferocious so far. She became the only Empress in history to succeed in enthroning her own Pope, Virgilius, in Rome in 538.

She had, in effect, ascended the papal throne in

person, and it is more than likely that this is the source of the legend of the mythical Pope Joan.

Before we turn our attention to the eyewitness accounts supplied by Procopius, it is fitting to preface them with one last excerpt from an independent source.

Among the accredited historians of Byzantine history of this era are three of importance—Agathius (530–582), John Lydus (490–565), and Evagrius (536–594). Evagrius in his *Ecclesiastical History* (iv. 32), makes this comment:

"There was also another quality latent in the character of Justinian—a depravity which exceeded any bestiality which can be imagined. And whether this was a defect of his natural character, or whether it was the outgrowth of cowardice and fear, I am unable to say, but in any case it manifested itself as a result of the popular Nika insurrection."

Here is a side of the Emperor which Procopius documents in detail, yet it is discreetly ignored in the standard references, most of which content themselves with discrediting Procopius outright and whisking a whitewash brush lightly across Theodora's diabolism.

THE SECRET HISTORY BY PROCOPIUS

The version of the *Anecdota*, or *Secret History*, from which we now quote is one of seven volumes which include the *History of the Wars* and *History of the Buildings* (Harvard University Press), translated by H. B. Dewing, Ph. D., L.H.D., in 1935.

According to Dewing, the personable and well-educated Procopius arrived in Constantinople from Caesarea in Palestine while still a young man. Almost at once he was appointed legal adviser and private secretary to the patrician Belisarius, Justinian's youngest and most illustrious General. This is hardly a privilege accorded an anonymous scribbler of salacious gossip.

Indeed, we are immediately confronted by an unexpectedly articulate and imposing figure, the official historian of Justinian's three wars against the Persians, the Vandals, and the Goths respectively, in which capacity he traveled in the personal entourage of Belisarius and observed the wars firsthand.

"Besides his intimacy with Belisarius," says Dewing, "it should be added that his position gave him the further advantage of a certain standing at the imperial Court of Constantinople, and brought him the acquaintance of many of the leading men of his day. Thus we have the testimony of one intimately associated with the administration.

"One must admit that . . . the imperial favor was not won by plain speaking; nevertheless we have before us a man who could not obliterate himself enough to play the abject flatterer always; and he gives us the reverse, too, of this brilliant picture (in) the *Anecdota,* or *Secret History.* Here he freed himself of all the restraints of respect or fear, and set down without scruple everything which he had been led to suppress or gloss over in the *History of the Wars,* through motives of policy.

"It is a record of wanton crime and shameless debauchery of intrigue and scandal, both in public and private life . . . we seem to hear one speak out of the bitterness of his heart. It should be said, at the same time, that there are very few contradictions of fact.

"It was the intention of Procopius to write a book on the doctrines of Christianity (and the long and often bitter debates, in the course of which these

189

were formulated), as he definitely states in Chapter XI 33 of the *Secret History*—a promise which he repeated in the eighth book of the Histories XXV. 13.

"It is most unfortunate that he was prevented from fulfilling this promise, for his point of view was that of a liberal who was puzzled by the earnestness with which his contemporaries entered into the discussion of these matters."

Even a cursory study of the War Histories reveals Procopius not only as a diligent and meticulous chronicler, but conscientious to such a degree that he was prepared to risk the ire of Justinian by rightfully crediting Belisarius with the success of the three campaigns.

If he promised to write a treatise on the religious confusion of the time, it is more than possible that he did write it. The fact that it is missing does not necessarily point to foul play by his enemies, when one recalls the widowed Lady Burton burning her husband's exotic translations from the Arabic "to keep his memory pure." Even so, we cannot ignore the fact that Procopius's *History of the Church* could have been so explosive in content that a timid bibliophile, discovering it on some forgotten shelf, would be impelled to deliver it into the hands of the authorities rather than offer it for sale to a private collector.

It was, after all, a private collector who discovered the *Anecdota* manuscript in Rome in the mid-nineteenth century. Written in Greek, and intact, it had obviously been lovingly protected for more than fourteen hundred years. But as far as we may ever know, the *History of the Church* vanished as utterly as the Imperial Court archives in Constantinople, which did not even survive the remorse-ridden senility of Justinian.

Those gifted with the patience to endure the

archaism of Procopius's style will find that a series of very real, convincing portraits will emerge from the *Secret History* as distinct from the expedient effigies which adorn the standard references. It will even become apparent that the accounts of Justinian's insomnia and schizoid outbursts have a disturbingly familiar ring. They follow the same behavior-pattern as Hitler's—a fact which would have been inaccessible to Dewing in 1935, the year he completed his translation.

A PORTRAIT OF THEODORA

Procopius supplies such a vivid first-hand account of Theodora's sexual promiscuity that most of it is too disgusting for inclusion here, although, when it is measured against the excesses of the more degenerate Caesars, it is credible enough. He then continues with a description of her after she became Empress:

"Now Theodora was fair of face and in general attractive in appearance, but short of stature and lacking in color; being, however, not altogether pale but rather sallow, and her glance was always intense and made with contracted brows. She lavished more care on her body than was necessary, but never as much as she considered adequate. For instance, she used to enter the bath very early and quit it very late, and go thence to her breakfast. After partaking of breakfast, she would rest. At luncheon and dinner, however, she partook incontinently of food and drink, so that sleep would constantly lay hold of her for long stretches of time, not only in the daytime up to nightfall, but at night up to sunrise, and although she indulged herself in every excess for so major a portion of that day, she still claimed the right to administer the whole Roman Empire.

191

"And if the Emperor should impose any favor upon a man without her consent, that man's affairs would suffer such a turn of fortune that not long thereafter he would be dismissed from his office with the greatest indignities, and would die a most shameful death."

All of which has the ring of firsthand reporting of a highly responsible order.

A PORTRAIT OF JUSTINIAN

Procopius then presents in detail his theory that both Theodora and Justinian were "possessed by demons." And here the same manic disorders that distinguished Hitler come into sharp focus, even if the language of that time lacked the advantage of modern psychiatric idiom:

"And I think it not inappropriate here to describe the appearance of this man. He was neither tall in stature nor particularly short, but of medium height, yet not thin but slightly fleshy, and his face was round and not uncomely, for his complexion remained ruddy even after two days of fasting. But his character I could not accurately describe, for this man was both an evildoer and easily led into evil, a perfect artist in acting out an opinion which he pretended to hold, and even able to produce tears . . . not from joy or sorrow, but contriving them for the occasion, according to the need of the moment . . . always playing false, yet not carelessly, but adding both his signature and the most terrible oaths to bind his agreements, and that, too, in dealing with his own subjects. . . .

"And they say that a certain monk who was very dear to God . . . set out for Byzantium in order to plead the cause of the people living near the monas-

192

tery who were being wronged in unbearable fashion, and immediately upon his arrival he was granted admittance to the Emperor. But just as he was about to enter his presence, having already placed one foot across the threshold, he suddenly recoiled and stepped back.

"Now the eunuch who was his conductor, as well as others nearby, besought him earnestly to go forward, but he, acting like a man who had suffered a stroke, made no answer but departed thence and went to the place where he was lodged.

"And when his attendants enquired why he had acted thus, he declared outright that he had seen the Lord of the Demons sitting on the throne, and had declined to suffer his presence long enough to ask anything from him.

"And how could this man fail to be some wicked demon, who never had a sufficiency of food, or drink, or sleep, but, taking a haphazard taste of whatever was set before him, walked about the Palace at unseasonable hours of the night, though he was passionately devoted to the joys of Aphrodite? He was not given to sleep as a general thing, and he never filled himself to repletion with either food or drink, but he usually just touched the food with the tips of his fingers and went his way."

Justinian's split personality is shrewdly and articulately observed in the following: "However, he did not, on that account, blush before any of those destined to be ruined by him. Indeed, he never allowed himself to show anger or exasperation, thus to reveal his feelings to those who had given offence, but with gentle mien and lowered brow, and in a restrained voice, he would give orders for the death of thousands of innocent men, for the dismantling of cities, and for the confiscation of all monies to the Treasury. And one would infer from this characteristic that he had the spirit of the lamb. Yet if anyone sought to intercede through prayers and supplications for those who had given offence, thus to gain for them forgiveness, then, 'enraged and shewing his teeth,' he would seem to be ready to burst, so that none of those who were supposed to be intimate with him had any further hope of obtaining the desired pardon.

"And while he seemed to have a firm belief as regards Christ, yet even this was for the ruin of his subjects. For in his eagerness to gather all men into one belief as to Christ, he kept destroying the rest of mankind in senseless fashion, and that, too, while acting with a pretence of piety. For it did not seem to him murder, if the victims chanced to be not of his own creed.

"And I shall show further, how . . . many other calamities chanced to befall, which some insisted came about through the afore-mentioned presence of this evil demon and through his contriving, while others said that the Deity, detesting his works, turned away from the Roman Empire and gave place to the abominable demons for the bringing of these things to pass in this fashion.

"Thus the Scirtus River, by overflowing Edessa, became the author of countless calamities to the people of that region, as will be written by me in a following book.

"And earthquakes destroyed Antioch, the first city of the East, and Seleucia which is close to it, as well as the most notable city in Cilicia, Anazarbus. And the number of persons who perished along with these cities, who would be able to compute?

"And one might add to the list Ibora and also Amasia, which chanced to be the first city in Pontus, also Polybotus in Phrygia, and the city which the Pisidians call Philomede, and Lychnidus in Epirus, and Corinth. And afterwards came the plague as well, mentioned by me before, which carried off about one half of the surviving population."

Substitute the Allied bombing raids of Germany in World War II for the natural disasters, and Hitler's "voices" for the demons which "possessed" Justinian, and the parallel is neither fortuitous nor farfetched.

Procopius has drawn two very real portraits, and it seems unconvincing to reduce his observations to malicious chatter.

THE FIFTH ECUMENICAL CHURCH COUNCIL

Theodora, having contrived the murder of two Popes, expected to instill their successor Virgilius with her own mania for exterminating all traces of the Chalcedonian Decree and its division of Christ into two separate entities, human and divine. She failed.

What caused her death no one seems to know for certain. The *Encyclopedia Britannica*, finally giving Procopius the benefit of the doubt, set the date as 547.

One thing is certain: Justinian continued to conduct his affairs exactly as if she still stood at his elbow. He was determined to deify her and himself by totally obliterating any facet of the Christian religion that might in any way disqualify such a grotesque conceit. What religious doctrine could possibly have deranged him more than reincarnation's dispassionate law of cause and effect? What other law could obliterate both his and his consort's imperial status at the moment of death, reduce them both to the common denominator of backward souls, and then bundle them back into lives of abject atonement to balance the scales?

Justinian's opening gambit was to disinter a tooth-less and forgotten civil law, passed in 531, called the Three Chapters Edict. This had lashed out indiscriminately at three long defunct heretical author-bishops, Theodore, Theodret and Ibar. This unimposing edict had apparently alarmed no one except Virgilius at the time; and now, in 553, his fears were fully confirmed when Justinain found it necessary to convene the lumbering weight of the Fifth Ecumenical Church Council to incorporate this very minor tempest in a teapot into canon law.

When he went so far as to exclude all but six Western bishops from the Council, while permitting the attendance of one hundred and fifty-nine Eastern bishops (all of 'them, presumably, faithful Monophysites), Justinian provoked Virgilius to belated but courageous action.

Pope Virgilius demanded that the Eastern and Western bishops be given equal representation, a demand that was promptly and predictably quashed by Justinian.

Robbed, thus, of his last shreds of superficial authority, Pope Virgilius refused to attend the Council, though his motive might have been less loyalty to the Vatican then self-preservation. Justinian was not above hastening his end with the same dispatch that had been meted out to Agapetus and Silverius.

If the Church of Rome had not been powerless to oppose the military supremacy of Byzantium, Virgilius could have forbidden Justinian to convene the Fifth Council on pain of excommunication. Again, if there had been a bit more of the stuff of martyrs in Virgilius, he might have aroused sufficient protest in the

West to make Justinian think twice, for the Emperor would have been in no haste to provoke a public uprising on the scale of the Nika insurrection of 523, which was still raw in his mind. Unfortunately, like Becket, his past was against him. He found himself at odds both with the ill-omened pyrotechnics of his master and his own conscience.

There is something stupefying in the haphazard lack of concern for the keeping of the Council's records. When the Council ended in an atmosphere suitably obscured by organized confusion and high-sounding bombast, Justinian officially announced that the Council's sole purpose in convening was to legalize the well-worn Three Chapters Edict, and that this was now accomplished.

Pope Virgilius was served official notice that the Three Chapters Edict was now law. And so, to all intents and purposes, the Council had fulfilled its declared function, and the Bishops departed.

Now the Three Chapters Edict, in itself, was very small political beer. If that had been Justinian's only concern, he could easily have had it incorporated into canon law without recourse to the elaborate machinery of a full-scale Ecumenical Council. This was like chopping down a whole orchard to pick one apple.

If, on the other hand, one of the Emperor's purposes was to delete all reference to metempsychosis from the original Gospels, he most certainly would have needed the imposing might of the Fifth Council to cloak his mischief.

What exactly were the real purposes of the Congress?

If one was to condemn the writings of Origen, the immediate effect would, of course, be the obliteration of the Chalcedonian Decree of 451. It is therefore imperative that we never confuse the Chalcedonian Decree of 451 with the ridiculous Three Chapters

Edict of 531; for the sleight-of-hand of the Fifth Council would deceive the eye in exactly this fashion.

Who really instigated the Council?

The unquiet wraith of Theodora. It was her posthumous coup d'etat to the autonomy of the Western Church in Rome. The Monophysites were henceforth to realign the Church from their Eastern stronghold.

In brief, concealed beneath all the pomp and circumstance of the Fifth Council there were some hidden agendas, and one victim was reincarnation in all its Platonist, Origenist, secular, and unsecular forms.

Yet, Emperor or no Emperor, Justinian was a layman tampering with ecclesiastical law. The titular head of the Roman Church had not agreed to calling the Council and was not himself present, although he later wrote a letter approving the Council, but with no mention of Origen. And only six Western bishops had been permitted to vote.

The findings of the Council did, of course, discourage Origenism in the Christian church. Though Origen was not condemned as a heretic in a formal way by the Council, the inclusion of his name in the list of heretics led many later Christians and even councils to think of him as heretical. A few stubborn sects, notably the Cathari or Albigensians in Southern France, went underground for a few more centuries, becoming active again in the 12th and 13th centuries.

Moreover, the condemnation of Origen in canon 11, the list of heretics, now stood revealed as an attack on all the early church fathers whose writings reflected their veneration of him. Copies of their works were not numerous and could easily be tracked down. The early Gospels were either in Latin or Greek, and were usually not allowed to fall into the hands of laymen.

Few, if any, monasteries would have had the courage to defy their Emperor and hide their original versions. Justinian's deletions and alterations of the

Gospels could have been completed in very short order and so could the elimination of all and any evidence of the vandalism.

Even so, certain questions remain stubbornly unanswerable. Surely, if Pope Virgilius had not felt assured that the Western church was solidly behind him, he would never have taken on Justinian. Yet he did oppose the Council.

If we are expected to believe that the full sympathy of the Western bishops was solidly behind the Monophysite dogma, why should Justinian have gone to such lengths to bar them from the Fifth Council? Surely he would have welcomed them in?

By what process did the Vatican eventually arrive at the conclusion that their Pope had voluntarily approved the anathemas and officially accepted them as canon law?

The absence of all but six Western bishops at the Council was hardly calculated to instill into the heart of the Mother Church a sudden trust in its bitterest foes, Theodora and Justinian. Was the Vatican prepared to submit to their intimidation for all eternity? Fear of Theodora's avenging arm is understandable during her lifetime. . . . but in his old age Justinian distintegrated into a demoralized dotard, repenting his ways and desperately seeking absolution. Why was the issue never reexamined by a properly authorized Ecumenical Council?

The *Catholic Encyclopedia* informs us that Virgilius and the four Popes who followed him give recognition only to the Three Chapters Edict when referring to the Council, and speak of Origenism as if they knew nothing of its condemnation.

Five hundred years later, in 1054, the Roman and Greek churches excommunicated each other. Surely no division of ideologies could be more total? But yet another puzzling aspect of the suppression is the ambivalence shown by the Greek church at the Council of Florence during the Renaissance. George Gemistus, attending as the Greek Church's deputy, urged Cosimo de Medici, then at the height of his power, to form a Platonic Academy in Florence. This served to introduce metempsychosis into European philosophy, even though the Church remained firmly uninvolved. Voltaire's caustic comment that "today Roman Catholics believe only in the councils approved in the Vatican, and Greek Orthodox Catholics believe only in those approved in Constantinople" implies an ironic reversal of loyalties to Platonism. Rome had to condemn it before the Greeks would condone it, even if they, too, still excluded it from their creed.

This is tantamount to saying that the real findings of the Council, never having been submitted to the Church of Rome, were therefore never ratified by it.

The Council had been no more than an elaborate thimblerig to conceal a much more intimate conclave which had been held in secret a few days earlier. In this secret cabala, according to the *Catholic Encyclopedia*, "the bishops already assembled at Constantinople had to consider, by order of the Emperor, a form of Origenism that had practically nothing in common with Origen, but which was held, we know, by one of the Origenist parties in Palestine."

The *Encyclopedia* concludes with the statement that the bishops obediently subscribed to the fifteen anathemas proposed by the Emperor against Origen*, and that Theodore of Scythopolin, an admitted Origenist, was forced to retract. But (and we may attach the most vital significance to the following) "there is no proof that the approbation of the Pope, who was at that time protesting against the convocation of the Council, was asked. It is easy to under-

* (See Appendix A)

stand how this extraconciliatory sentence was mistaken, at a later period, for a decree of the actual ecumenical council."

For whom is it so easy to understand?

During the nearly fourteen hundred years which have elapsed since the Council, no ecclesiastical authority has subjected the problem to examination, or even evinced the slightest desire to do so.

Head and Cranston in their *Reincarnation, An East-West Anthology* supply this cogent summing-up: "It seems clear that. . . . Catholic scholars are beginning to disclaim that the Roman Church took any part in the anathemas against Origen; suggesting that during the many centuries when the Church believed it had condemned Origen, it was mistaken.

"However, one disastrous result of the mistake still persists; namely, the exclusion from the Christian creed of the teaching of the preexistence of the soul, and, by implication, reincarnation."

CHAPTER TWELVE

THE SALEM WITCH TRIALS: THE "PURITAN ETHIC" IN THE AMERICAN PSYCHE

It is understandable that references to the Salem Witch Trials of 1692 are given special emphasis in the Life Readings, in that they were the first examples of religious persecution to leave their indelible stains both on the New World and the human souls who were involved.

Fourteen men and five women were hanged, and one man was pressed to death for refusing to plead innocent or guilty. Fifty-five others only escaped by turning informer on the innocent, and when the authorities finally regained their sanity, a hundred and fifty people were still languishing in jail.

Here again the "scars stretch down the centuries." The overall impression conveyed by the Readings is that among the innocent men, women and children who were persecuted was a core of devout visionaries and genuine clairvoyants.

Most significantly, the cases which appear in the Cayce files are nearly all linked in some way with psychic problems in the present. In this first example we find physical and emotional karma converging again.

Some thirty years ago an A.R.E. member requested urgent help for her sister, Moira Schaeffer. A struggling artist of thirty-three with a shy, introspective and somewhat self-pitying nature, Moira had been invited to a Greenwich Village party where she was to meet "artists and dealers who would help her forward her career." She eventually returned home in a state of traumatic shock which deteriorated so rapidly into self-inflicted violence that it was necessary to confine her to an institution for the insane.

In her delirium she constantly cried out in terror that someone was trying to hurt her, and was in abject fear that she would be visited again by "the man with the black umbrella."

Her Life Reading regressed her to New England at the time of the witchhunts. Here Cayce found her as Mana Smyrth, possessing to a minor degree a talent for clairvoyance which swiftly brought her to the prisoner's dock. Her sentence was comparatively light. She was condemned to a series of public witch-duckings. But such duckings were often brutal enough in themselves to cause accidental drowning, and Mana Smyrth emerged from her ordeal embittered and vengeful.

"The Entity suffered under those persecutions, and often was brought under submission by the experiences of ducking.

"Thus the Entity inherits both good and bad influences from same in the present. Here we will find the needs for definite stands to be taken. While the Entity is afraid of water in a sense, we find that water—or color and water—must be a manner or a means or a channel for the greater expression."

The intensity of her hatred and anger canceled out whatever gains she might otherwise have made by forgiving her enemies. By thus abusing the Law of Grace, she found herself enmeshed once again in the karmic laws of cause and effect, where a deal of unfinished business awaited her from a life as an artisan in a distant Arabian incarnation. "Much disturbance physically and mentally arose through that period," Cayce told her, "and yet—as the Entity found, even then—a greater outlet for her abilities to depict the beautiful in art. So may she find the same in the present."

Despite this note of hope, the case remained a stubborn one in all its aspects. Moira's Physical Reading indicated that damage incurred in her spine was causing the insanity, but it was difficult to persuade the hospital authorities either to remove her from the violent and incurable" ward or authorize osteopathic adjustments. Her weight was down to eighty pounds. In her total derangement she recognized nobody. However, Edgar was so vehement that she must be helped at all costs that David Kahn, a senior A.R.E. member in New York, used all the authority he could bring to bear. And after a long and laborious succession of appeals and minor miracles the girl was eventually restored to sanity and health by the aid of osteopathic treatments.

Her career as an artist took on full stature when her Reading told her that she had once been an apprentice in the atelier of the famous artist Peter Paul Rubens (1577-1640), and that if she hewed closely to his school of painting, her own style would evolve successfully. Her letter of gratitude to Edgar Cayce contains this touching excerpt: "I feel so much happier in spirit since I received the Reading. It seems incredible that any human being could see and feel things the way you do! The Rubens influence has been noticed in my work before, which makes this very convincing; I shall study up on Rubens's work and period, which I have already done, to some extent, in Boston. . . . Rubens was a master of the oil. As for the water color, it is peculiar the way things arrange themselves. I have always been somewhat afraid of a lot of water, and yet, as you said in the Reading, that's where water-color painting comes in."

No evidence was ever forthcoming of the exact nature of the outrage to which she was subjected, but her sister's impression, having listened to her delirium, was that a malign form of hypnotism had been used prior to the most brutal molestation.

If this was indeed so, could there be a boomeranging here of a revengeful Salem "witch" cursing her tormentors with more potence than she herself knew she possessed? And did she thus catch herself in her own trap? For to curse another "is to be cursed by self."

Two worthies appear in the Readings whose existence can be confirmed, though it should be born in mind that spelling in those days was often arbitrary and phonetic—John Dane, who took part in the general persecution, and the Rev. James Allen, a pastor who attempted to defend the persecuted.

John Dane (or Dain), was "among those who first landed in that country now known as Massachusetts and among those called the Puritans. The Entity gained through service rendered to others, and through the application of self to the (spiritual) building in body and mind; for the Entity endured much suffering during that period."

An interesting sidelight to this incarnation is the Reading's reference to Dane's previous life as an English monk who had allowed "the weaknesses of

206

the flesh" to cause him to break his vows. He was obviously atoning for it in his life as Dane.

At least two books contain historical reference to him as a member of the jury which tried the so-called witches: *More Wonders of the Invisible World*, published by Robert Calef in 1700; and *Witchcraft* by Charles Williams, published by Faber and Faber, London, in which is an account of how a group of jurors "signed a statement wherein forgiveness was asked for having had a hand in the persecutions." Among these names was that of John Dane.

The Reverend James Allen was a minister both in Salem and in Providence Town, "and there may be found yet, in the outer-portion of Salem, the monument, or the little slab, here of Allen, the minister of this church."

The Reading states that Allen was persecuted for his attempt to defend those of his parishioners who "had come to a free land that they might worship their God according to the dictates of their own conscience.

"Yet the Entity within itself gained throughout the experience. Though banished, he was loved by all those whom he served in body and in mind during that sojourn, bringing to self in his latter days the commendation of all that had known of the persecutions he had undergone.

"And to this Entity, this is the test of the fidelity of the soul even in the present."

Allen's existence is confirmed in *Records of Salem Witchcraft*, Vol. 2, by Elliot Woodward, but the graveyard where he was buried has been allowed to go to ruin. Even so, according to the Reading, his own headstone is still intact and decipherable, even if it is now part of a wall or a vestry floor.

Both these men fared well in their present lives, having retained the compassion and tolerance they exercised during the persecutions. Even Dane, though he had sat on the hanging jury, had dared to be as just as he could, and more than one poor creature must have owed her life to the vote Dane cast in her favor

THE CROWS COME HOME TO ROOST

Next we come to the complex case which might have derived from the pen of Poe or Hawthorne. In the early thirties, the Reading of Ezra Brandon, aged thirty-five, married with a young family, overlapped that of Marion Kramer, spinster, a few years older than himself.

Brandon was suffering from psoriasis, brought on by a back injury, but his Physical Reading had done much to alleviate it.

Marion was dabbling actively in the arcane Possessing a slender gift for genuine clairvoyance she was "spreading it around" by a dramatic use of automatic writing and impressive sessions with the ouija board. Her nature was restless, mischievous; her regard for the feelings of others, nil. When she met Ezra Brandon she developed a sexual obsession for him to which he responded. Directing her concentration to his weaknesses, she soon befuddled him with her dominating personality: the ouija board assured him that they were "soul mates" who belonged together, and urged him to free himself of his marriage ties. The merest modicum of truth underlay her theatrical sleight of hand, but it was enough to hook and gaff the credulous Brandon.

Both of them disregarded the warnings implicit in their Readings. Brandon divorced his wife and deserted his family. The moment he and Marion became man and wife, misfortune, which had till then remained in abeyance, descended on him. Not only did his livelihood crumble under a series of disasters, his ill-health returned, never to leave him again and eventually to bring his life to an end.

On the face of it, this was the kind of dreary tragedy that occurs every day at all levels of society. But in this case it was the playing-out of an unsavory relationship which had begun in Salem nearly three hundred years before.

There the couple were again man and wife, but the man, as Jacob Bennet, persecuted the women accused of witchcraft with unwholesome zeal, making no exception of his wife when she was discovered to be one of the victims "and oft was dipped—and once put in the stocks—for her activities."

Both Marion Kramer and Ezra Brandon had returned with positive potentialities. Marion was told that her ability could have been constructively channeled into some form of lay-therapy, working in conjunction with psychoanalysis or psychiatry, and Ezra was told that his remorse for his intolerance in Salem might be easily directed towards social and religious work in this life.

What reshackled them to each other, and wrecked their present lives, then? Clearly the incapacity to forgive, on Marion's part—the desire to be revenged for the cruelties in which her husband had played so large a part as Jacob Bennet. By reverting to a life in Greece which she had wasted gratifying the flesh when she had possessed unusual physical beauty, she had used a purely sexual coercion to entrap him.

And why had he passively allowed her to tear his life to pieces? He had been on the mend physically; he had not been unhappily married. It was almost a passive submission to destruction. No free will was used; indeed, it was abused. In this atmosphere of

209

arid nihilism, the Law of Grace could not exist: therefore both of them were left to the tender mercies of the law of cause and effect.

THE GOOD FRIENDS

Yet good could come out of Salem, and never more surely than it did in the following relationship. It concerns a married woman and her brother-in-law, both by the name of Alden. He was the assistant to a stool-dipper, but found his task so thoroughly repugnant that he finally declared his sympathy for the oppressed. In the woman's case, "she suffered in body for the persecutions brought to her household. Hardships came upon the Entity, and she held grudges against those who had brought suffering to her loved ones.

"In the present there has ever been an innate awe of those who are teachers, ministers, or any who profess association with unseen sources," and a dread that they might come to harm for expressing their true opinions.

Had she been accused of witchcraft by association? The innocent invariably suffer twice as cruelly as the guilty in times of public persecution, and seldom if ever receive redress. Whatever the case, she was running a boarding house in Norfolk when she was made welcome by Edgar Cayce because of the intense sincerity of her power to pray. As a member of the A.R.E. prayer group, she developed the rare ability to "heal with her hands."

In this life, her brother-in-law was born a German national, and as a teenager he served as an infantryman in World War. I. During the final defeat of Germany he was badly wounded and left to bleed to death on a deserted battlefield. Throughout the

ight, however, his wounds were staunched and he
was kept alive by a luminous supernatural being. This
he took to be his Guardian Angel—(and his is by no
means a rare example of this type of phenomenon
in the 1914-18 war)—for he was one of the first of the
wounded to be discovered by the stretcher-bearers in
the early dawn of the following day.

Subsequently he emigrated to America, and fate
took him surefootedly to the boarding house in Norfolk where he was warmly welcomed by the sister-in-
law of the old Salem days, now a widow of fifty-eight.
Through her, he obtained a Reading from Edgar
Cayce and even studied at the ill-fated Atlantic University which was organized in conjunction with the
Edgar Cayce Hospital, and which likewise foundered
with the '29 crash.

Cayce was able to clarify that the young man's
Guardian Angel was not an angel in the scriptural
sense but one of the Watchers, or Helpers, who have
made sufficient spiritual progress to be able to come
to mortal aid while they themselves are in the next
dimension, awaiting rebirth.

This advanced soul had been able to repay, in full,
the pity and kindness that Alden had shown to the
victims of persecution in Salem. This is as good an
example as any of the Law of Grace in action, super-
seding all the lesser laws of karmic cause and effect.

Another positive note is struck in the case of the
woman who had escaped from Salem to Virginia as
the Witch, Jane Dundee," and though harassment
and rejection of one sort or another followed her even
here, she steadily continued to do what good she
could until her death. Her Reading informed her that
she had been one of the sick children healed by Christ
during His lifetime, and that the desire to heal had
persisted throughout the balance of her lives, defying

the hangman's noose in Salem and manifesting now in a power to "heal with her hands."

The overall impression given by the references to Salem in the Readings is that the soul-group which incarnated there had shared a cycle of reincarnation which included France (from the Crusades to the Revolution) and Palestine in the time of the Master, then Greece, prehistoric Egypt and the cryptic and forbidding continent of Atlantis. Those souls who had responded instinctively to the preaching of Jesus tended to display strong spiritual fiber and courage during the Salem trials. Where and when they could, they strove to bring back sanity and tolerance.

Those who came to grief in Salem often had a record of intolerance, beginning in Atlantis, that led directly to their misfortunes in Salem. But it is cheering to observe how many profited by their mistakes and returned to the twentieth century prepared not only to live and let live, but to make themselves useful to their fellow men.

One captures vivid flashes of Salem's effect on a particular soul by such haphazard references as these:

... "The Entity was then one Sally Dale, who lost her life through the cold caught by dipping" .. accounting in the present for her fear "ever to allow herself to express fully that which she feels within when dealing with such subjects as witchcraft."

... "In the name of Marie Smith ... heard and saw visions that were the imaginings of a mind far from home (this refers to the tall tales of a West Indian slave woman) who had heard in the groaning of the forests a sign that the souls of people live on.

"In the present, this may bring a curiosity, a wanting to know—yea, the listening to snatches of conversation not too nice—for oft ye will hear that which, if left unheard, would have made thee much happier!"

... "In the name Elsie Pepper . . . being among those who defied those who, as termed by Him, were wolves in sheep's clothing. Thus the interest in the present in all things of that nature (witchcraft)—and no wonder have there been the dreams and visions!"

... "The Entity was one Bill Edmundson, who made light of, yet experienced those close associations with earthbound spirits, or Entities, who had not found the Way. Yet the Entity put same aside, without analyzing or doing much about same. The Entity was then a storekeeper closely associated with some of the Ministers and councilmen . . . thus we find that commercial interests, the ability to speak in public, and those things pertaining to occult or psychic forces, are a part of the present experience. And all these things have their place, but the Entity must not become too rabid, or censor without due consideration of others. For freedom of speech does not entitle any individual to speak ill of his neighbor. Rather, it gives one the privilege of being a constructive influence through one's speech, thought and actions. And thus is freedom free indeed, as truth makes it so!"

... "During the persecutions of those who had familiar spirits, or those who saw, heard and understood much that is closed from material-minded men; the Entity was considered too lenient with those of the opposite sex as shared such experience, and suffered both in body and mind. In the present (the memory of) such experiences causes shudders in the region of the pineal and its center, as of shivers, quivers, or quakes; and sorrow enters in the mental being. These, if applied in the service of an ideal, may become worthwhile."

... "The Entity persecuted those who had visions or dreams, or those who were considered to have familiar spirits. Yet when those of his own household

213

were counted among those who had seen visions and
heard voices, the Entity found confusion even in self.
Hence in the present there may be seen the interest
in things of a psychic, occult or scientific nature.
However, these but confuse. Beware of mysteries that
may not be practical in the material experience, but
beware as much of those who would make their soul
—or psychic—experiences so practical as to impede
the spiritual development of the soul itself!"

"A SORT OF SADDUCEE"

A certain mystery arose over a Salem life attributed to an A.R.E. member, "then in the name of
Robert Calvert. The Entity made for many questionings, and acted in the capacity as a judge in the tenets
of the very orthodox relations of church, of state, of
people."

The recipient of the Reading obligingly wrote the
following to Gladys Davis Turner:

"For a matter of months, I searched the records
for a Robert Calvert who fitted the description. The
only representatives of that name in the New World
were associated with Maryland, not Massachusetts.
There was no Robert among them, and the line did
not extend beyond the originals themselves, they being unmarried and having no heirs.

"The index of *The Devil in Massachusetts* revealed
no Robert Calvert, but it did list a Robert Calef,
whose character and activity fitted exactly with the
details presented in the Reading.

"He was a Boston merchant, rather deprecatingly
referred to as a weaver, who most assuredly made for
many questionings and acted in the capacity of judge.

"The discrepancy of the name is easily accounted
for as an error in transcription, since the shorthand

symbols are quite similar, and substituting a familiar name for one unfamiliar would seem natural enough. I believe no one would hesitate to say that Robert Calef was the man whose record was referred to.

"He was born in England in 1648 and came to Boston sometime before 1688 with his family. Two of his eight children were born after his coming to Boston, his eldest son being in 1693 a physician in Ipswich. In addition to his business and his justifiable meddling in the witchcraft matter, Calef was from 1692 to 1710 a constable, hayward and fence viewer, a surveyor of highways, a clerk of the market, an overseer of the poor, an assessor, and a tithing man! He retired to his own property in Roxbury, Massachusetts, where he died and was buried in the old burial ground opposite his home, April 13, 1719, aged seventy-one.

"He seems to have been one of the few sane heads in the place, and weaver or cloth-merchant though he was, he did not hesitate to make his own observations and draw his own conclusions. Nor did he hesitate to question repeatedly the decisions, theology, and reasoning of the two Mathers, Cotton and Increase. And, when they failed to give him satisfaction, he appealed to the clergy at large. He followed Cotton Mather's *Wonders of the Invisible World* with a book of his own, *More Wonders*, which was five times reprinted and is today recognized as the work of a mature and fair-intentioned individual possessed of an orderly mind.

"I shall forgo inordinate self-praise (although I am inclined to it) that father Increase, as President of Harvard, burned this man's book in Harvard Yard, and son Cotton called him 'a sort of Sadducee in this town.' And to have called the true infantile and fanatic character of these two divines to the fore is in itself a mead of praise and a modicum of comfort!

"Maybe I'm presumptuous and overhasty, but I'm

proud of Robert Calef—he's just the kind of man, not only that I should have liked to be, but the kind I still want to go on being for some time to come!

"It might be harder, however, for another to see the connection between what Cayce says of the virtues and vices appertaining to Calef which still show in the present personality. But I feel they are there.

"'Hence those influences in the present in which the Entity finds that he almost attains, and yet there is an influence or a force apparently outside or beyond his control . . . for as the Entity measured to others, so the Entity meets self in the present.'

"The exact explanation of anything is as important to me as ever. Although today not even as successful as a cloth merchant; and being wholly inexperienced as a surveyor, hayward, constable, or overseer of the poor; I still will take issue with anyone, so far as keeping the record straight. And I want to get it down on paper too, in just the way I see it—step by step—even at the expense of seeming tedious and pettish!

"Furthermore, I'm still unregenerate and a trifle stiff-necked: I'm a libertine in Puritan garb—and the 'Mathers' of this world and I are still at odds! Maybe they were right, and I am a sort of Sadducee!"

CHAPTER THIRTEEN

THE REPERCUSSIONS FROM THE SEARCH FOR BRIDEY MURPHY

The three men who have done most to popularize Edgar Cayce's approach to reincarnation are the late Thomas Sugrue, who knew and loved him like a son; Morey Bernstein, who came to Virginia Beach after Edgar Cayce's death with the express intention of exposing him as a fraud; and, most recently, Jess Stearn.

Sugrue obviously needs no introduction here, and Stearn's book, *The Sleeping Prophet*, speaks for itself.

Bernstein was an intense, dedicated young man of independent means, whose medical study of hypnosis eventually led him to *There Is A River*. In Pueblo, Colorado, he discovered a young housewife, Ruth Simmons, who was so susceptible to hypnotic suggestion that he was able to regress her to the life of an Irish peasant woman who had lived in Belfast in the first half of the nineteenth century.

Bridey Murphy was thus destined to relive an obscure and uneventful existence in full view of the American public, and for a few years she reigned as queen of the newspaper headlines.

In 1956 Bernstein published *The Search for Bridey Murphy*, an account of the hypnotic sessions. In his favor it should be said that Bernstein was utterly unprepared (as were the rest of the people involved) for the best-selling overnight sensation the book became. He was likewise unprepared for the pained reaction such a vulgar success aroused in the more conservative echelons of the various Establishments; and retribution was swift to descend on his head.

For a while, the furore aroused by the book threatened to bring disrepute to everybody concerned, even those remotely involved in the proceedings. And because Edgar Cayce was featured in the first third of the book, the aims of the A.R.E. could have suffered a public setback if the drive against reincarnation in all its forms had succeeded in its aims.

For this reason the Bridey Murphy incident warrants more than a passing nod in the present volume.

In his zeal to get the full story, he presented his questions with the impartiality of a district attorney determined on getting the truth out of a recalcitrant witness, quite forgetting that the I.Q. of an uneducated servant-type of the early 1800's had less than nothing in common with the I.Q. of Ruth Simmons.

Bridey, on first being allowed to express herself, was more than delighted. She gossiped happily, flattered to be the center of an attention she had never enjoyed in the flesh. She was anxious to be liked and to make a good impression, and she was naturally reluctant to expose herself as an illiterate peasant. She promoted her husband and her family to the lower-middle class she had obviously always held in wistful awe and envy. (Actually, she must have been as low down the scale as the wife of a coachman or the messenger for a Belfast solicitor.) Her boasting, alas, while only human and certainly forgivable, crumbled under the lie-detector methods of Bernstein.

As one listens to the tapes, one becomes aware of her gradual bewilderment, and then her active fear, as she finds herself being grilled by "hostile members of the upper class." The little white lies she had told were thrown back at her, implying that nothing she had said was being believed. With her reluctance to be exposed and made a fool of, a sympathetic reluctance began to evidence itself in Ruth Simmons on a subtler scale. She began to chafe at the imposition made by the sessions on her own life, and Bernstein was reduced to having to beg her to continue.

It is significant that on all the minor details that an uneducated servant could be expected to know, Bridey was checking out well. She correctly named shops in the town, the popular reading matter, (which she personally could never have read), the type of meals she served, the colloquialisms for domestic articles, and distinctly expressed her awe of Father Gorman, the parish priest, apparently a rather distant young cleric with waning hopes of better things than an impoverished parish. The stark, arid loneliness of existence of the poor in that century comes through the tapes in sober measure. Bridey had almost no pleasures to speak of, and a great deal of unrewarding slavery. She died of sheer exhaustion, prematurely old, cowed in death as she had been in life, unable to make her presence known to her senile husband and equally unable to progress beyond the primitive astral world that clutters the outer perimeter of life. In this "purgatory of the under-privileged," life-after-death took on the thought-form drabness of a workhouse or almshouse in permanent twilight. And in one of his less diplomatic moments, Bernstein included in the book Bridey's reference to a meeting at this level with Father Gorman, as dazed and disorientated as herself. (This, of course, offended the sensibilities of our present-day clerics who were later to denounce the book from their various pulpits.)

Two most affecting phenomena must be given mention here. As Bridey's uneasiness and bewilderment with Bernstein's cross-examination increased, she resorted more and more to pitiful attempts to mollify him. She would develop a convenient cold which caused her to cough when his questions became too aggressive, or she would complain that her foot was hurting from a sprain incurred in dancing an Irish Jig.

Then, towards the close of the sessions, as the questions centered more on Bridey Murphy's last years, a voice emerged from Ruth Simmons that not even the most accomplished actress could have simulated. It was the slack-throated, utterly weary half-whine of a sixty-year-old woman, resigned to speaking with a toothless palate and now completely reconciled to abject poverty and physical misery. The accent was confined to the flat, inimitable vowels of the Belfast slum—an accent that has never crossed the Atlantic, in that it is never used by American actors. (All this was preserved on tape.)

If Ruth Simmons had been a vocal genius, she would still have had no means of re-creating these accents consciously. And Ruth Simmons was not a passably adequate amateur actress.

The behavior-pattern of Bridey on these last tapes is more convincing than fifty technical proofs that such-and-such a street existed in Belfast at that time, or whether Bridey as a child referred to her bed as an "iron bed" or a "foine bed."

If Bernstein had been the sly fox the press called him, he would never have been so naive as to publish his book before he had accumulated a solid backlog of evidence. And to obtain that evidence, he would first have had to permit a trained and tactful psychologist to do the questioning of Bridey, and he would have had to bury himself for at least six months or a year in Belfast, up to his ears in the records of the nineteenth century.

Even if he had done all this in overwhelming measure, it is still anybody's guess whether the book's reception would have been any more open-hearted.

The facts have been objectively analyzed and presented by C. J. Ducasse, Professor of Philosophy Emeritus, of Brown University, Rhode Island in his book, *A Critical Examination of the Belief in a Life after Death*, published by Charles Thomas, Springfield, Illinois, 1961.

In it Professor Ducasse devoted thirteen objective and impartial pages to the Bridey Murphy controversy which are required reading for anyone even mildly interested in the Hallowe'en hubbub after all these years.

Professor Ducasse quietly and sanely put the matter into perspective as no one else has been able to do. He defended Bernstein and came to the support of Ruth Simmons, whose real name was Mrs. Virginia Tighe of Pueblo, Colorado, exonerating her from all suspicion of fraudulent practice.

Mrs. Tighe was born April 27th, 1923. At the age of three she was adopted by an aunt, Mrs. Myrtle Grung, and grew up in Chicago. At the age of twenty she married a U.S. Air Force flyer who died in action a year later.

Virginia's second marriage was to Hugh Bryan

Tighe, a Denver businessman, with whom she had three children. As both her husband and her own relatives were "very much opposed to the whole Bridey phenomenon on religious grounds," Virginia was unprepared and unequipped both for the sensationalism the Bernstein book aroused and the backlash that curled around her family's defenseless heads.

Life magazine began to zero in on Bernstein as early as March 1956, but it was the *Chicago American* which fired on Fort Sumter. In June it began a series of skeptical articles, using as its authority a Rev. Wally White of the Chicago Gospel Tabernacle, who had vowed to "debunk reincarnation because of its assault upon established religious doctrines."

White claimed to have known Mrs. Tighe from her childhood, but she herself stated that she had never met him until he appeared uninvited at her door in 1956 and informed her that it was his duty to pray for her soul.

The *Denver Post* came valiantly to the defense of Virginia and Bernstein, but its guns were silenced when *Life* dealt the coup de grace on June 25 with a summary of the *Chicago American's* exposé, and a photograph of a certain Mrs. Bridie Murphy Corkell and her family, of whom more later.

As fascinating a piece of Freudian curiosa as any that emerged at this time was a book jointly written by three New York psychiatrists, which had as its purpose the total annihilation of the theory of reincarnation forever. This book, *A Scientific Report on "The Search for Bridey Murphy"* came to a singularly unscientific end as a discount bookstore remaindered it at forty-nine cents a copy.

Of the Rev. Wally White, Professor Ducasse has this to say: "It would seem, then, that the featuring of this clergyman's name at the head of several of the *American's* articles was just psychological window-dressing for the benefit of pious but naive readers. Such readers, seeing articles under the by-line of a clergyman, and having been told that he is the pastor of the church Virginia attended in Chicago, would naturally assume that he has firsthand knowledge of her childhood and youth; that his articles are based on that special knowledge; and therefore that, since clergymen are truthful, the articles bearing the Rev. White's by-line must be authoritative. But although the reader is likely to infer all this from the articles, they carefully refrain from actually asserting any of it.

"The climax, however, of the *Chicago American* series of articles was the discovery of a Mrs. Bridie Murphy Corkell in Chicago, who lived across the street from one of the places where Virginia and her foster parents had resided, whom Virginia knew . . . but although the articles state that she 'was in the Corkell home many times,' Virginia never spoke with Mrs. Corkell—nor does the article assert that she ever did.

"Further, Virginia never knew that Mrs. Corkell's first name was Bridie, and still less that her maiden name was Murphy, if indeed it was. For when the *Denver Post* tried to verify this, Mrs. Corkell was not taking telephone calls. And when its reporter Bob Byers inquired from her parish priest in Chicago, he confirmed her first name was Bridie, but was unable to verify her maiden name as Murphy; nor could the Rev. Wally White do so.

"But the reader will hardly guess who this Mrs. Corkell, whom the *American* 'discovered,' turned out to be. By one more of the strange coincidences of the case, Mrs. Bridie (Murphy) Corkell happens to be the mother of the editor of the Sunday edition of the *Chicago American* at the time the articles were published!"

The farcical aspect of the whole story only emerges in full relief, however, when we examine the fate of the film version, which was already in production at Paramount Studios with Pat Duggan as the producer, when the storm signals were run up the mast.

The screenwriter-director of the film reports as follows: "In the screenplay, I was limited to the material Bernstein had published in his book, though there was far more dramatic and convincing material elsewhere on the original tapes. The climax of the picture was carefully constructed to scare the public off the irresponsible use of hypnosis as a party-trick, and I even wrote in a gratuituous scene where a Protestant minister and a Catholic priest gave their definitive opinions on the theory of reincarnation (subversive paganism), and hypnosis (for the birds).

"The salaries budgeted for the two principal actors were modest to say the least, but I managed to blarney Teresa Wright into such enthusiasm for the role that she agreed to work for the allotted pittance. So did Louis Hayward, who, because of his earlier costume pictures, had become inexcusably underestimated as an all-around character actor. The studio heads, instead of evincing pleasure at the casting, went out of their way to show the back of their hands to both stars, and only the fact that I am six-foot-five preserved me from having to carry a loaded fly-swat to defend myself in lonely corridors. Nevertheless, I soon began to call our unit the 'Contamination Ward.' My production manager had been privately informed by higher sources that the picture would never be finished, but that Duggan and I already were. My cutter, a gregarious type, spent happy hours on the stage disparaging the filming, but none, as far as I could gather, in the cutting room . . . nothing I was shooting would 'cut together.'

"We were able to defend the picture from open

sabotage on the studio floor, but when it became necessary for us to use the special-effects laboratory —we had 'ghost' sequences and intricate mechanical dissolves from modern Colorado to Ireland in the 1860's—we were informed that Mr. De Mille had commandeered the effects lab in toto for "The Ten Commandments." We then requested that the rushes be sent to an independent effects lab outside the studio. We were told this was quite impossible. Finally my cameraman, Jack Warren, put the clock back fifty years and did all the double-exposures right on the set, using nothing more complicated than a prism, a mirror, and a two-foot strip of plain glass, lamp-blacked at one end, greased with Vaseline in the center and clear at the other end. This, when drawn slowly across the lens of the camera, was twice as effective as a modern lab dissolve.

"The worst, however, was yet to come. *Life* magazine had been paying close attention to the Bridey Murphy craze for some time, tracing its pernicious influence to teenage parties where irresponsible young 'beats' regressed equally irresponsible young girls into presumable seductability by the gross. Halfway through the picture, *Life* broke the story that the whole thing was a hoax.

"Our budget was low and we were bringing in between four to ten minutes of screen time a day (this with adequate covering shots), but from the Contamination Ward we were relegated to the Leper Colony. There was a move afoot to suspend production entirely, and I found myself not only directing but holding the bridge like Horatio, which at least kept the foe at bay during working hours. We brought the film in on time, but less than five minutes of it had been cut. I managed to get the cutter replaced at the eleventh hour, and in the short cutting time left to us, we had to protect Teresa's performance first—once that was in balance, we would have been able to bring Hayward's performance up to match it. He had worked with unselfish intensity, and Teresa's performance reflected his team-work; but it would have taken another week to cut him into the picture in his proper stature, and we were denied that extra week.

"Even in its maimed and limping state, the film got a round of applause at its sneak preview in a particularly rough and unresponsive neighborhood theater in Glenwood. This should have heartened the executives sufficiently to let us finish the job, if only to protect the shareholders' investment, but I never saw the film again.

"When it was released, the general press gave it the silent treatment and it obediently wilted on the vine.

"No one in Hollywood ever saw it, in case their presence in the audience could be interpreted as subversive malfeasance, yet Duggan and I were treated as renegades who had gratuitously smirched the proud heritage of the Four Freedoms."

It is a far cry from the uneasy fifties to the success of Alan J. Lerner's Broadway musical in 1966, "On A Clear Day You Can See Forever." The intervening years had seen the theory of reincarnation advanced in the public mind from a scaremongering bogey to a sedate muse, perfectly at home on the Broadway stage and responding happily to the warmth and charm of Lerner's genius.

The majority of the critics found it a little too defiant of orthodoxy to be treated cordially, but the audiences established their own standards, much as they will during a newspaper strike. In fact, the house was sold out for six months in advance when the show opened at the Mark Hellinger Theater.

Briefly, the plot deals with a modern Trilby, Brooklyn model, who is a natural hypnotic subject for a personable young psychiatrist. He regresses her to an earlier life in eighteenth-century England, and it is implied (though never flatly stated) that he was her inconstant lover in that period.

The psychiatrist proceeds to fall in love with the English belle, Melinda, while her contemporary edition, Daisy, falls in love with him, to their mutual frustration.

In her life as Melinda, the heroine had perished while escaping to America on the sailing ship Trelawney. Fleeing from her psychiatrist, Daisy almost meets the same fate by booking a flight on a transatlantic jet—also called (why not?)—Trelawney.

Representing the popular misconception of reincarnation is the Greek shipping magnate, Kriakos, who offers the psychiatrist a fortune to tell him who he will be in his next life, so that he can will his millions to himself in advance.

Daisy's ESP and the course of true love save the day. Ultimately she permits her previous personality to move in and "take over the management" of her present self. But before the happy ending, the audience has been treated to a painless but thorough grounding in the advances ESP has made in the last decade. Lerner contents himself with saying in effect: all this will soon be acceptable to society; this is the psychiatric logic of tomorrow.

In the November, 1965, issue of *Atlantic Monthly* is an interview with Mr. Lerner, in which the dramatist states: "Somebody asked me if I thought (the play) was a fantasy, because it touched on the possibility of reincarnation, and I said, 'Well, no, not to five hundred hundred million Indians it isn't!' . . . .

"The only surprising thing about (the play) is that I haven't written it before. Extrasensory perception has been my hobby all my life. . . . I know, of

227

course, that only twenty-two percent of our brain is in practical use. The rest of it must be doing something up there besides filling out the hat. I've never had any extrasensory experiences myself, except for one minor one when I was writing 'Brigadoon.'

"The first act of 'Brigadoon' ended with a wedding, which had to take place outside the church. I tried to figure out why in seventeenth and eighteenth century Scotland anyone would be married outside a church, and if they were, what the ceremony should be. So I figured something out and wrote it down.

"Several years later I was in London . . . and I stumbled upon a book called *Everyday Life in Old Scotland*—and there was my wedding ceremony, word for word! . . .

"When I began to think seriously about why I wanted to write a musical about (reincarnation), I realized that in recent months I had become increasingly outraged at all the pat explanations psychoanalysis was throwing up to explain human behavior. I was becoming more and more disgusted by the morality of psychoanalysis—that we are living in a world where there is no more character and where everything is behavior; that there is no more good, it is all adjustment; that there is no more evil, it is all maladjustment. Psychoanalysis has turned into a totally unsatisfactory religion which gives no life hereafter, and no divine morality to live by. And so I began to think, 'Well, yes, this might be a good thing to write about.' I would find a way of saying I don't think that we are all that explainable; that much of us is still unknown; that there are vast worlds within us, and that it's a thrilling possibility to contemplate."

1966 also saw the publication of Dr. Ian Stevenson's *Twenty Cases Suggestive of Reincarnation*, which we will examine next. Here we find reincarnaion afforded the full dignity of acceptance by a distinguished professor in the Department of Neurology and Psychiatry of the School of Medicine at the University of Virginia.

CHAPTER FOURTEEN

THE WORK OF DR. IAN STEVENSON

Dr. Stevenson, heading the vanguard of responsible investigators seeking firsthand evidence of reincarnation, has journeyed as far afield as India, Ceylon, Lebanon and Alaska. In 1966 he published his findings under the title of *Twenty Cases Suggestive of Reincarnation.**

The singular characteristic of the Eastern cases is the brief interval between the souls' death and the rebirth. While the Cayce Readings roughly measure rebirths in terms of centuries and half centuries, in Dr. Stevenson's cases the average is nearer ten years or less . . . sometimes instantaneous, as in the case of a Hindu youth of twenty-two, poisoned to death by a debtor, who reincarnated into the body of a three-and-a-half-year old boy, presumably dead of smallpox. The boy revived, but from then on identified only with the characteristics and history of the twenty-two-year old, even to the extent of correctly describing his former family, and recognizing each one individually when taken to see them.

---

* Published by the American Society for Psychical Research; New York, 1966.

The most compelling example, in that Dr. Stevenson was able to observe it while it was still occurring in Lebanon in 1964, concerned a five-year-old Arab boy named Imad Elawar, living in the village of Kornayel. Before he was two he had begun to refer to his past life. His first words referred affectionately to his mistress of his previous life. Imad was fortunate to possess parents who did not subdue his chatter with the severity such children usually receive. Born December 21, 1958, he claimed to have lived in his former life, in the village of Khriby, some twenty-five miles away, as Ibrahim Bouhanzy, who had died of tuberculosis on Sept. 18, 1949. Imad correctly supplied the dying words of Ibrahim, correctly identified the surviving members of Ibrahim's family, and never ceased to refer affectionately to Jarmile Ibrahim's mistress. Ibrahim's village and house were likewise familiar to Imad. Dr. Stevenson traveled with Imad and his family to Ibrahim's village, and tabulates the fifty-seven items recalled from memory by the child as follows: "Of the fifty-seven items, Imad made ten of the statements in the car on the way to Khriby . . . of these ten, three were incorrect. Of the remaining forty-seven items, Imad was wrong on only three items. It seems quite possible that under the excitement of the journey . . . he mixed up memories of the 'previous life' and memories of the present life."

As much as it was possible to verify the evidence of the two families, Dr. Stevenson did so meticulously. Most of the proof was immediately self-evident. Neither family stood to gain, and both stood to lose by lying, in that it could not be denied that the child's memory had been correct fifty-one times out of fifty-seven.

Dr. Stevenson points out that if there had been collusion between the two families (who were unnown to each other until they met to satisfy the child), the motive would have been hard to establish. No family would assiduously accumulate evidence so reluctantly over so long a period for the mere sensationalism of getting their name in the papers. Indeed, Dr. Stevenson's reception by most of the Hindu families he interviewed was hostile, at first.

In the case of the "possession" of the three-and-a-half-year-old "corpse" of Jasbir by the twenty-two-year-old discarnate Hindu youth Sobha Ram, the embarrassment to the family of the child Jasbir was further aggravated by the child's refusal to eat anything except Brahmin food, which had to be prepared and cooked for him by a sympathetic Brahmin neighbor. Anyone familiar with the implacable ferocity of the Hindu caste laws will comprehend that a Jat child would normally sooner starve than eat Brahmin food, no matter how unbalanced his mental faculties might otherwise have become. It is also hard to conceive of a child of Jasbir's tender years suddenly behaving with the articulate authority of a youth eighteen years his senior.

"During my stay," writes Dr. Stevenson, "I easily noticed that he did not play with other children, but stayed aloof and isolated. Yet he talked willingly with my interpreter, although wearing always a sad expression on his quiet, pock-marked but handsome face."

The Brahmin family of the dead Sobha Ram were willing to treat Jasbir hospitably, but his own Jat family deeply resented his identification with a family of superior caste, and their opposition to the "previous" family of their son reached its zenith in their dogged refusal to let him meet his own "widow."

"Readers may wish to know, as I did," concludes Dr. Stevenson, "what account Jasbir gave of events between the death of the Sobha Ram personality and the revival of Jasbir (from his presumed death) with memories of Sobha Ram.

"To this question, Jasbir replied in 1961 that after death he (as Sobha Ram) met a Sadhu (a holy man or saint) who advised him to 'take cover' in the body of Jasbir.

"Although the apparent 'death' of Jasbir occurred in the period April-May 1954, close to the identified date of Sobha Ram's death, we do not know that the change in personality of Jasbir took place immediately on the night when his body seemed to die and then revived.

"In the following weeks Jasbir was still perilously ill with smallpox, barely able to take nourishment, and not able to express much of any personality. The change of personality may therefore have happened quickly or gradually, during the weeks beginning immediately after the apparent death of Jasbir."

In terms of documented evidence, this case is unique. In most instances of this nature, the soul is given time to depart from its adult body before its next body is conceived, even in cases of violent death.

The allusion to the "holy Sadhu" who directed the discarnate Sobha Ram to "take cover" in the dead or dying body of Jasbir suggests a state of emergency, a breakdown in the normal "laws of creation." Edgar Cayce has admitted that "sometimes there are mistakes, even in the firmament"; even though they are too rare to be placed in the category of hazards. He has also suggested that the first astral plane i primitive, in that it distortedly resembles the earth plane, and can be inhabited by the thought-forms o backward or undeveloped souls, able to assume al the menacing outward trappings of the nightmare.

If we assume that Sobha Ram's premature and un expected death as a result of poisoning was not an ticipated in the karmic laws to which he conformed

234

it might well have left him vulnerable to some hostile and vengeful soul who had been awaiting just such an opportunity to square accounts with him.

In his own state of disorganized confusion, unable to defend himself, one of the more benign Helpers or Watchers could have appeared to him in the reassuring form of a Sadhu and shown him the only sanctuary available—the uninhabited shell of the dead child. This could have been purely a temporary measure, until the immediate danger on the lower astral had been deflected and Sobha Ram could proceed safely to a more enlightened and protective level. (Here again we employ Cayce's argument that the forces of evil, no matter how stubborn or of what intensity, can always be dispersed by prayer from a pure and responsible source.)

It could be possible, however, that once Sobha Ram had reentered the material confines of human flesh (rather like a lobster crawling into a lobster-pot), he was unable to extricate himself again; and is now compelled to remain "earthbound" as Jasbir until he has lived out the requisite number of years still due him on his own karmic record. Mercifully his memory of his previous life will gradually fade.

REINCARNATION IN THE FROZEN NORTH

The Eskimos of northwest Alaska, the Aleuts to the west, and the Tlingit Indians to the southeast, all base their religious beliefs on reincarnation. The Tlingits further personalize it by believing that souls return to their own immediate families.

Between 1961 and 1965 Dr. Stevenson made four visits to the Tlingits, obtaining thirty-six claimed cases of reincarnation. These cases were not difficult to collect, as most of the Indians spoke English and many of the claimants bore "sympathy" scars in the present life which identified the manner of death in the previous life.

In 1949, a Tlingit Indian fisherman of sixty, called William George, told his son and daughter-in-law he would return as their son. He promised them they would recognize him by his present birthmarks, and gave them his gold watch for safekeeping. A few weeks later, he disappeared from his seine boat without trace. Barely nine months later his daughter-in-law gave birth to a boy "who had pigmented naevi (moles) on the upper surface of his left shoulder and the volar surface of his left forearm at exactly the locations mentioned by the grandfather."

As he grew up, the boy displayed a behavior-pattern similar to his grandfather's, even extending to a physical limp which his grandfather had incurred in a basketball game. Before he was five, the boy identified his watch by picking it out of his mother's jewelry box unprompted, and stubbornly maintained his right of ownership. He referred to his uncles as "sons" and his great-aunt as "sister."

Dr. Stevenson wrote: "He shows a precocious knowledge of fishing and boats. He also shows greater than average fear of water for boys of his age. He is more grave and sensible than other children of his group."

Even more evidential is the case of another Tlingit, Victor Vincent (tribal name, Kahkody), who died in 1946.

In the previous year he had told his favorite niece and her husband Corliss Chotkin that he would return as their child, and promised that they would recognize him by the scars he bore—one on the side of his nose and another on his back, the remains of an operation that still revealed the marks of the stitches.

Eighteen months later Mrs. Chotkin gave birth to

a son who possessed birthmarks which exactly duplicated Vincent's scars. At thirteen months he interrupted his mother's efforts to teach him his name, Corliss Chotkin Jr., by asking: "Don't you know me? I'm Kahkody!"

At the age of two he correctly identified his previous stepdaughter Susie, his son William, and his own widow. He continued to exhibit unusually detailed recall until the age of nine, from which age his memory began to fade, finally becoming inactive in his fifteenth year.

Dr. Stevenson tabulates each case meticulously and academically. He states his own views, doubts and rationalizations in great detail. Nevertheless, his book emerges as a responsible assembling of incontrovertible facts. In his conclusion, he makes no claim to having proved reincarnation, but the evidence for it has never been presented by a more responsible spokesman.

CHAPTER FIFTEEN

THE LAW OF GRACE

Obviously, the simplest way to illustrate the Law of Grace is to show it in action.

Anthony Hollis had fallen in love with a girl while he was still in college in Connecticut. He lost her to his best friend without a struggle, and his subsequent Reading told him his subconscious memory had stood him in good stead: twice before in the past he had been married to her, and twice before she had been unfaithful to him. The Reading even specified a life in ancient Egypt in which she had run off with the same friend! It did not offer details of any other life with her, beyond the implication that violence and tragedy had always dogged them.

Hollis had taken full advantage of his opportunity to receive further Readings, and as he had put their morality into practice to the best of his ability, he could justifiably be called a "good Christian." He married well and the college infatuation was soon buried and forgotten. In 1944, he was called to active service and took his training as a transport officer at Fort Custis, Va.

One day he happened to swallow a plum pit which

lodged so firmly in his throat that he had to report to the hospital to have it removed. He thought no more of it at the time. But while he was based in England prior to the D-Day invasion of Europe, he choked again, this time on a piece of gristle. Once more the situation was serious enough to warrant medical aid. By this time it was too late to request a Reading from Edgar Cayce, and by the time Anthony Hollis experienced his third mishap in occupied Germany, Edgar Cayce was dead. Each mishap was more serious. In Germany he was all but strangled by a segment of bone from a stew.

Back in America after the war, he was dining with a friend in New York City, when a chicken bone lodged in his throat. He was rushed to hospital, where an inexpert doctor wasted valuable minutes trying to give him a barium test "to prove that the choking was psychosomatic."

When they finally rushed him to the operating table, Hollis was barely conscious, yet while they were working on him with oxygen masks and local anaesthetics, he found himself confronting a strange, vindictive face framed in straggling locks of dirty yellow hair. He was thrust deeper into this level of consciousness until he "merged" with the other personality and discovered it to be himself. The surroundings vaguely suggested a Nordic environment about nine or ten centuries back . . . and he was confronting a young woman. His grief and rage were homicidal; he knew she had been unfaithful to him. He knew she was his wife, but that was all.

At exactly the time this was happening, a friend of his in San Francisco received a vivid "photo-image" of this same demented face and associated it with Hollis. In this hallucination, however, no woman was present. Hollis was chained to a dungeon wall, one of a group of unkempt, ragged men. The impresion was sufficiently vivid for his friend to phone Hollis the next day in some consternation. When Hollis and his friend compared notes, no shred of doubt remained that they had both seen the same face.

Hollis searched his Readings but could find no specific reference to the "fellow with the dirty yellow hair." The Readings had emphasized the karmic trait of a quick temper that Hollis at all times went to great pains to control. In Edgar Cayce's cautious, tactful notes, there were allusions to karmic debts still to be paid. The Readings made a great point of suggesting that instead of pursuing the "eye for an eye, tooth for a tooth" law of literal restitution, Hollis should attempt the more enlightened method of evening-up his reckoning by forgiveness and prayer.

This seemed a complicated task for a man in the twentieth century who had apparently hated a woman in Viking Norway in the eighth or ninth century. But the matter was taken out of Hollis's hands. Less than a week later he dreamed the same macabre dream. This time the unfamiliar features of the woman took on the "ghost" physiognomy of the girl who had jilted him in college, and he was strangling her in deadly earnest. On the split-level he now occupied between dream and karmic reenactment, Hollis began to pray with all the intensity and faith he could muster. He prayed for the spiritual strength to forgive the woman he was strangling; he prayed for her to be forgiven her adultery; he prayed for himself to be forgiven for having strangled her to death. Anyone who has literally prayed his way back from deathbed will confirm that, once it attains to a certain intensity, genuine prayer manifests as energy that surmounts all other factors opposing it.

When Hollis woke the next morning, he was aware of a weight gone from his mind, a sense of newly found freedom he had never known before, and the feeling remained with him over the balance of the week. Yet he had no tangible means of assuring himself that his prayers had freed him permanently from the karmic yoke that had hung so heavily around his neck. Not, that is, until his phone rang on the Saturday, and he heard the voice of his victim in the dream.

She had long divorced his friend and married again. Her second marriage had also foundered; and now, a rich woman, she wandered the world on luxury cruises with her children, disconsolate and unfulfilled. For no reason at all, when her ship docked in New York, she found herself thinking of Hollis with remorse for the way she had jilted him, and her phone call a whim. "I do hope you've forgiven me by now? I did treat you so disgracefully!"

In a heartfelt burst of relief and gratitude, Hollis fervently assured her that he had forgiven her a thousand times over!

What would Hollis's karmic alternative have been? Surely an increase in the intensity of his choking fits, until one killed him. The debt he owed was to himself, for having once committed murder. The fact that in this life the girl, herself, spared him the misery of having to marry her again, and that he then suffered the same miserable ordeal of her betrayal, did not take him off the karmic hook. The murder had still been committed; the Law still demanded that it be accounted for. Thus, when the freedom of his throat was in any way obstructed, the symptoms of his physical response were of strangulation, not ordinary choking.

But his outward decency toward the girl in the present; plus the fact that once Cayce had explained the karmic cause, Hollis bore her no grudge and wished her no ill, worked in his favor. As soon as hur pride and outraged vanity had been removed from the picture, the complications vanished also, and he was left to face a clear-cut test.

The source of the will-power and concentration Hollis was able to apply to his final prayer of forgiveness is defined very simply in the following words: "Yet it is a fact that a life experience is a manifestation of divinity. And the mind of an Entity is the builder. Then, as the Entity sets itself to accomplish that which is creative, it comes under the law which operates between karma and grace. No longer is the Entity under the law of cause and effect, or karma, but rather, in grace, he may go on to the higher calling set in HIM."

"To be sure, the law applies," said Cayce in a similar situation. "For in the beginning of man, in his becoming a living soul in the earth, laws were established, and these take hold. But do not lose sight of the law of grace, the law of mercy, the law of patience as well. For each has its place—especially when individuals desire to be channels through which God may manifest."

THE NEEDLESS DESPAIR OF A RESOLVED SOUL

The second case is that of Vera Aldrich, housewife, aged fifty-three. Here we see the error, made by an advanced soul whose path has been almost too physically hard to bear, in assuming that her karmic debts have demanded their reckoning, and that she is about to be visited by her old guilts.

"Why should I come into this life with such a broken physical body? It seems I have been through hell (but an interesting trip so far!) and I have often wondered what I have saved myself for. I have always wanted to be of service to humanity, but had no

243

strength . . . angina, pernicious anemia, and so on since I was young. Why did I bring such a broken body to live in? Have I committed a great crime in the past?"

Cayce's answers were couched entirely in warm reassurances.

"This Entity was associated with the one who persecuted the church so thoroughly, and who fiddled while Rome burned (Nero). That's the reason why this Entity has been disfigured by the structural conditions of the present body.

"Yet this Entity may be set apart! For through her experience in the earth, she had advanced from a low degree to the point where another reincarnation in the earth may not even be necessary.

"Not that she has reached perfection, but remember, the material, and material urges, exist in other consciousnesses, not in just the three-dimensional. . . There are other realms for instruction, if the Entity will hold fast to the ideals of those at whom she once scoffed (the Christians in Rome).

"There is more that might be said, but we would minimize the faults and we would magnify the virtues. And little or nothing could be given that would deter the Entity in any way, for, as Joshua did of old she has determined that 'others may do as they may, but as for me—I will serve the living God!'

"As to the abilities: Who would give glory to the morning sun? Who would tell the stars how to be beautiful? Keep that faith which has prompted thee Many will gain much from thy patience, thy consistency, thy love!"

This woman, by her generous and unselfish way of life, had achieved Grace without even realizing it at the conscious level. Her long karmic wanderings were over.

"To be sure, individuals grow in grace, in knowl

244

dge, in understanding, and as they apply that which they know, the next step is shown to them. . . . For His promise is: 'I will be with thee always, even unto the end of the world.' He was with thee in the beginning. Ye wandered away. . . ."

Gladys Turner Davis, Edgar Cayce's permanent secretary from 1923 to his death, transcribed nearly every Reading in the files, not once but five times over, and has remained as selflessly loyal to him as he was in his lifetime. No other member of the A.R.E. possesses her unique familiarity with the Readings, and perhaps no one else exemplifies so unobtrusively the application of the laws of Grace to everyday existence. She considers it was a rare occasion when he told someone their soul was so far advanced that they need not return to earth again.

On one of the rare occasions when she was persuaded to express herself on paper, she pays Edgar his tribute:

"During Mr. Cayce's lifetime, I can remember only three instances in which the individuals claimed their Life Readings were incorrect—only three out of nearly 2,500!

"Since Mr. Cayce's death, in gathering progress reports to index with the Readings, we have encountered only one unfavorable report—from a mother who complains that there was 'nothing personal' in the Reading for her six-year-old daughter.

"It has happened time and again that Life Readings for children were put away and forgotten by the parents, then, later, were found to be true in every detail. But let us think for a moment about these few instances in which the Readings were disclaimed. Even if one in twenty-four had been completely wrong—that is an unheard of percentage in the field of psychic research—perhaps in any line of research!

"Those of us who know from experience the value

of these Readings are not only privileged, but in fact obligated, to press on toward perfection, carrying a torch not just for the theory of reincarnation, but for the whole Christian way of life as taught by Him 'Who, being in the form of God, thought it not robbery to be equal with God.'

"But what do the Readings mean to the millions who didn't even know or care that a man gave his life for them? What will it mean to the generations to come?

"It has been said that in the eyes of two or three witnesses, a fact is legally established. We have over two thousand living examples of correct analyses of capabilities and character based on akashic records of past lives.

"By a careful analysis and study of them, many of us are convinced that we can reach an understanding of the basic factors which govern man's thoughts and feelings. For these Life Readings represent interpretations of fundamental spiritual laws, applied, it is true, to personal problems. By studying a number of examples, we should be able to learn how to apply those same laws to our own personal problems."

CHAPTER SIXTEEN

GROUP KARMA

THE SURVIVORS OF FORT DEARBORN

Edgar Cayce, in his former life as the frontier scout Bainbridge, had ranged the newly-emerged nation of America from the Canadian border to Florida, an amalgam of pioneer hero and the Gaylord Ravenal type of riverboat gambler-gallant.

The crossroads of his various sorties had been Fort Dearborn, a trading post on the site of present-day Chicago. And it was here that he made his strongest ties with his fellow men. Fort Dearborn was rough terrain, perpetually on guard against hostile Indians, and the inhabitants worked and played hard. The Puritan element was present, but cheerful lip-service paid to virtue (a legacy from Jacobean England) was still the norm, and the trading post had its full quota of taverns, gambling-dens and bawdy houses.

The memory of this life was still so vivid in his own day that Edgar still regretted Bainbridge's persuasive tongue and easy charm with the ladies, and the wasted opportunities he had left behind him. Cayce never gambled for any stakes or any reason, and seldom if ever took a drink.

Bainbridge forged a strong emotional bond with Fran Barlowe, the daughter of the petit-bourgeois storekeeper of a minor trading post nearby. She was one of a large, neglected and turbulent family, and at the age of seventeen she was more than grateful to elope with a young tavern keeper of dubious worth and settle in Fort Dearborn. The tavern was merely the front for gambling rooms which specialized in bilking the sucker. It was Bainbridge's favorite haunt during his periodic stop-overs.

Fran developed no mean talent as a singer and dancer in her husband's tavern. She forged a close bond with the good-hearted madam of the girls of easy virtue, a woman who concerned herself with the welfare and health of her charges "over and above the demands of duty." Fran also crossed swords with a conscientious priest who viewed her and her frivolous associates with a bleak eye, reserving his particular disapproval for a convivial sexton who prayed piously by day, cut a nimble caper in the dance halls by night, and also found time to court the priest's sister—a romance which that worthy very rightly nipped in the bud, to the chagrin of the lovers. Toward the end, Fran began to mend her ways and severed some of her more disreputable ties, but "the sounds of revelry by night" were only silenced for good when the Fort suffered a mass Indian attack that burned it to the ground.

Bainbridge—who had previously been as willing to fiddle while Rome burned as the best of them, despite the great good he had done as a scout in the surrounding countryside—rescued one of the larger groups of survivors and brought them safely to the Ohio river, where a large raft of logs was hastily assembled to ferry them to the eastern shore.

Hostile Indian tribes pursued them along the eastern shore, however, and Bainbridge had no choice but to head down river to seek a safe landing. Unable to gó ashore to forage for food, even under cover of night, the exhausted occupants of the raft soon began dying of starvation and exposure, Bainbridge among them. But he had been able to keep Fran alive, and when the raft finally went aground she fell into the hands of friendly Indians and eventually made her way to Virginia. There she began life afresh.

By 1812, Fran was the proprietress of a modest boarding house where her warmth and kindness earned her the nickname of the Ministering Angel. She died at the age of forty-eight, honored and respected, the indiscretions of her youth apparently absolved and forgotten. But the life cycle in Fort Dearborn had not had time to complete itself. The scattering of the families by the Indian attack had left a deal of untidy and unfinished business.

Within seventy years, Fran returned to the self-same state of Virginia, where some of her competitors from Fort Dearborn had already begun to reassemble. As if by some tacit prearrangement, they had chosen the Chesapeake peninsula, within comfortable commuting distance of Virginia Beach, though Cayce himself was not to move there until 1925.

Fran soon found cause to feel she had been born under an unlucky star. She had made an early and disastrous first marriage and topped it with another, before the depression era of the early thirties found her on the run from herself in New York City, "slinging hash" in a workmen's cafe in a semi-slum district.

More benumbed than embittered, lacking confidence and direction, she had resigned herself to living from day to day with no real hope of finding her place in a world that seemed to consist of booby traps and built-in disillusions. It was here that David Kahn spotted her.

Kahn was the man who did more to bring Cayce to the attention of the people who needed him than any other single individual in the psychic's life. His business took him across the length and breadth of the eastern states and the middle-west, and wherever he went he extolled the powers of his best friend, Cayce, with eloquence and conviction. A garment-district hashhouse was not a usual port of call for him, but business having taken him there, he observed Fran shrewdly as she served him, and finally asked her the equivalent of "What's a nice girl like you doing in a dump like this?" When he learned that she lived near Norfolk, Virginia, he scribbled Edgar's address on a slip of paper and suggested that when she returned home, she apply for a Reading.

Fran figured she had better things to do with her money. Life had to apply a couple of more twists of the screw before she finally presented herself at Edgar's door a year or so later. He seemed to recognize her at once, and the atmosphere of peacefulness and calm radiated by the house and its occupants was the first real sense of sanctuary she had ever experienced in her twenty-five years.

There followed one of the most singularly compact series of Readings covering one soul-group. Nearly every member of Fran's large family was represented in it. Edgar felt he owed them reparation for the happy-go-lucky manner in which he had viewed their problems in Fort Dearborn.

Fran had been born back as a daughter to the madam who had befriended her in the Fort Dearborn days. Cayce cured her mother of a potential eczema, and she died at eighty-seven of nothing more toxic than "weariness of soul." Her father was likewise aided by Cayce to conquer a disgorged liver and an over-toxic blood count, and lived to be ninety. Her eldest brother Ned had also been her brother in Fort Dearborn. Joel, the second brother, had been the sexton who courted the priest's sister, and he had met and married that same sister in his present reincarnation. The marriage was a model of mutual happiness until the priest, true to character, incarnated as their first-born. As soon as he could express himself, his parents were never again to know an unharassed moment. Even as a very young child he played one against the other with such precocious zeal that he finally drove a permanent wedge between them. Singularly, he too, suffered from a third-degree skin disease that was finally cured by his Health Reading in his twenty-first year.

One of the most thoroughly documented of the Health Readings traces her sister Vera from advanced TB, diagnosed as incurable by her doctors, to total recovery with the aid of Cayce's "unorthodox remedies." Vera, secretive by nature, refused a Life Reading, perhaps fearing that her TB had been contracted in the dance halls of Fort Dearborn.

Fran's third brother, Hal, was fondest of her, protective, avuncular, and admiring. He loved to encourage her to sing and entertain, and would sit enraptured, applauding at the end and extolling her talents to the skies. Who was he? Her tavern keeper husband from Fort Dearborn. When he watched her conversion to the somewhat restraining standards of behavior laid down for her in her Readings, he developed an illogical antipathy for Cayce that he never overcame, refusing to meet him or even discuss him. His wife Sarah had no such mental block, having been one of the women whom Fran had nursed during the war of 1812. It was not until their first baby was three weeks old, and in such desperate need of expert medical help that was locally unavailable that her death seemed inevitable, that Hal, stonefaced, presented himself to Fran and asked her to get a Health Reading on the child from "that quack."

Fran explained that Cayce would only give a Reading if personally requested by the parent, but this far Hal would not go. At Fran's own request however, Cayce, aware that they had to fight the clock to save the child, broke his rule. The solution to the gastric problems of which the baby was dying was simply to dilute the formula and administer a dose of Castoria. Recovery was all but instantaneous, and three days later the baby was in perfect health, never again to suffer the same symptoms until colitis developed later in her childhood. This, too, was cured by a Reading.

Of the twenty or more Fort Dearbornites who had all reassembled in the Chesapeake peninsula, Hal and one of Fran's three husbands were the only who held out implacably against any aid, comfort or cheer that the Readings might have had to offer them. Actually Fran's second husband had not entered Fran's previous life until she was settled in Virginia, where he too, had been nursed back to health in her boarding house.

During the War of 1812, Fran had made no distinction between friend and foe when she administered to the wounded. Thus, as Fran reestablished her own life on a more stable footing, the chips on her shoulders fell away and her whole family group began to improve in health and self-orientation. The feuds diminished and the tensions abated. The old "unfinished business" of Fort Dearborn was all but accounted for.

Then a Mary Barker arrived on the scene to open a small gift shop for the summer tourists. Mary, not much younger than Fran, suffered from a form of polio which had given her an obese and crippled body. She had been unable to walk unaided since the age of one. From the moment she met Fran she developed an almost neurotic obsession for her, haunting her in her leisure hours and overwhelming her with clumsy affection.

Fran overcame her resentful embarrassment and obtained a Health Reading in the hope that Mary was still not beyond medical aid. The Reading prescribed a series of massages that were far beyond Mary's means. By this time she was well-nigh incapable of earning an adequate living. From a deep-rooted sense of compassion, Fran's mother took Mary into her house and for three months Fran applied the daily massages and packs. The girl slowly rallied and was eventually able to walk. She then requested a Life Reading which informed her that she had been Fran's daughter in the life before, and had suffered malnutrition when the Indian servants had fled with her to save her life. In adulthood she had been an itinerant barnstormer and rolling stone, convinced that her mother had willfully deserted her. Her unforgiving bitterness and self-pity had manifested themselves in the form of the disfiguring polio. When she finally moved away to pursue her career elsewhere, she and Fran were able to part as good friends.

Today Fran is a dignified matron looking fifteen or twenty years younger than her real age because of her strict adherence to her Health Readings. She shows understandable discretion when she discusses the benefits derived from the Readings by her family and friends. They, like many solid citizens who owe their equanimity and longevity to Cayce, are timid about admitting his help in public, lest some newspaper reporter descend on their heads for being arrayed as "a host of witnesses, almost none of them

253

named, who were snatched from certain decay by
the diagnoses that Cayce delivered in his trances.

Group karma does not apply only to a select few
who follow the same soul-cycle and reincarnate into
the same families; it has more universal implications.
Edgar Cayce made it abundantly clear that all the
souls involved in the Conquistador invasions of
Mexico and South America by Cortez and Pizarro
paid proportionately for their plunder and slaughter
of the Aztecs. This annihilation of an entire civilization is sickening to read even now; but the gold-
hungry adventurers, said Cayce, returned en masse
to Spain during the period of the Spanish Civil War
in this century. There, brother and mother and father
and sister turned against one another until their
civilization was a shambles. Does this throw a clearer
light on the reason why certain groups of apparently
innocent people are subject to undeserved horror and
tragedy?

Whole races seem to move with their soul-cycles.
It would seem that in contemporary America Negro
leadership is guiding the race toward its inheritance
of long-denied economic and social rights.

How then can we account for the unforgiving
hatred of the small minority groups such as the
Muslims; when we place it against the responsible
and disciplined rationale of the majority of the Negro
leaders?

It is possible that such implacability, far from re-
flecting the Negro group-cycles, stems rather from
an intrusion into the Negro race of souls who hate
Negro and white man with equal intensity? Such
souls could well have belonged to the reversionist
type of slave-owner in the ante-bellum South who
subjected his slaves to brutal floggings and ill-treated
their wives and children. Such souls would com-

pulsively have condemned themselves to reincarnate as Negroes: but while the erstwhile slave-owner's dark skin in the present might inflame his conscious grievances, his subconscious mind could be equally inflamed by the guilt and shame he feels for the crimes he once committed against the Negro race to which he now belongs; making him hate them as much as he does the whites.

CHAPTER SEVENTEEN

THE PRESENT ATTITUDE TOWARD REINCARNATION

1. THE PUBLIC

If the reader should question why reincarnation seems to thrive more in the Oriental and primitive societies, let him compare the permissive and tolerant upbringing of, say, a Tlingit Indian child with a child born into Colonial Salem possessing an equal aptitude for recalling its previous life. This would instantly be labeled as the work of the devil and zealously exorcized. Some of the women who were hanged were hardly more than children.

Such horrors are inevitably assimilated by what the great psychiatrist Jung calls the "collective unconscious" of an entire nation. And when a race contracts such infections of the psyche, taboos retard its intellectual reason for generations to come. In his grim play "The Crucible," Arthur Miller points the clear lineal descent from the mass hysteria of the Salem witch trials to the "monkey" trial of John T. Scopes for teaching evolution to his class in the twenties, and the un-American Activities Committee hearings of the early fifties.

If a brilliant scientist, educator or politician can be kept from assuming his rightful place in the affairs of his country by coercion, surely it is easy to see how children who believe the evidence of their own eyes and ears (and presume their parents do also) can be brainwashed into disowning their own psychic potential. A child who sees and talks to a very tangible replica of a dead grandparent, and is rash enough to say so, runs the danger of either being ridiculed, punished or sent to a child psychologist. It is inevitable that he will be reduced to repressing the evidence of his own spiritual senses until they atrophy.

2. THE CHURCHES

America, the youngest and strongest democracy ever to exist in the world's history, has proven capable of assimilating hostile idealogies and learning from them—provided a lunatic minority is restrained from harassing the level-headed majority. The brutality of Salem, for example, led directly to the inclusion of freedom of all worship in the Constitution.

If the Constitution is the rock on which democracy survives, then surely, when the Rev. Wally White vows to debunk Bridey Murphy "because reincarnation is an assault on established religious doctrines," he is just as misguided as his Salem forerunners.

What are the "established religious doctrines" that he and his ilk are always in such a fluster to protect? And how weak are they, that the protection of the Constitution is insufficient for their needs? Surely the faults in the established churches are more likely to resemble those criticized by Pope Pius XII in 1950: "We cannot abstain from expressing our preoccupa-

ion and our anxiety for those who . . . have become
so engulfed in the vortex of external activity that
they neglect the chief duty of the Christian: his own
sanctification.

"We have already stated publicly in writing that
those who presume that the world can be saved by
what has rightly been called the 'heresy of action'
must be made to exercise better judgment."

Fourteen years later, His Eminence Julius Cardinal
Dopfner, the fifty-one-year-old governor of the See
of Munich, defined the state of western religion today
in terms so brilliantly lucid as to make it definitive.

Cardinal Dopfner's prestige is such that he was
chosen by Pope Paul VI to be one of the four
Moderators of the second session of the Vatican
Council in 1964. In this capacity, he made pronounce-
ments to an audience of twenty-eight hundred people in the Congressional Hall at Munich. Of this,
Time magazine reported:

"Masses of the faithful have been lost, said
Dopfner, because to many the Catholic Church appeared as 'an institution that enslaved freedom' and
as a 'superannuated souvenir from the past age.' It
spoke to man in an ancient tongue, through incom-
prehensible rituals, in preaching concepts that have
no relation to current life. Instead of penetrating the
world, the church seemed to sit 'in a self-imposed
ghetto, trying to build its own small world adjoining
the big world.'

"Tied to 'antiquated forms,' Catholicism often gave
the appearance of resenting the inescapable presence
of idealogical pluralism, political democracy and
modern technology.

"These unpleasant truths persuaded Pope John
XXIII that the council was needed, and gave new
force to the traditional understanding of Catholicism

as *ecclesia semper reformanda*—a church ever in need of reform.

"Christ himself was free of sin, but the continuation of His work, Dopfner pointed out, 'has been entrusted to frail, sinful humans.' Thus the church has sometimes been guilty of 'failing to achieve what God had desired. The presentation of the love of Christ can lag, if the church uses the means of power instead of humility—of force instead of service.'

"This means, according to Dopfner, that any reform can only be carried out by the church at the council in a spirit of penitence, or metanoia, in the knowledge that it is 'a community of sinners.' Reform also must be based on the teachings of Christ and Holy Scripture. It also must be in the nature of renovation rather than revolution, preserving what is good from the past tradition while remaining open to future possibilities of development.

"We are in danger of resisting ideas, forms and possibilities to which perhaps the future belongs; and we often consider as impossible that which will finally manifest itself as a legitimate form of Christianity,' said the Cardinal.

" 'Even in the area of church teaching, development is far from impossible,' said Dopfner, since 'a dogma as such is not finally synonymous with divine truth, but only incompletely expresses the wealth of divine truth, because it sees revelation in human terms.'

"This does not mean that the church can recant or change dogmatic definitions of the past, but it can discover new aspects of truth, and find new ways to express traditional teaching.

"Thus the ancient belief of Catholics that 'outside the church there is no salvation' can be amplified to make it less offensive to Protestants. It should also be modified to recognize 'that the word and grace of God is effective in many manifestations outside the church.'

"To recognize this in a statement by the highest teaching authority is undoubtedly an innovation which, in earlier times when the people of other faiths were merely considered in the light of formal heresy, would have been utterly inconceivable.

"'But,' said the Cardinal in his peroration, 'the recognition of the Holy Spirit outside the limits of the Catholic church establishes a bridge to our 'separated brethren' and enlarges the order of the church as such. . . . This we view as the first step of the road along which God can ultimately lead us to each other.'" (*Time*, Feb 4, 1964).

These words resound with a somber magnificence because, in essence, they apply to all denominations where intolerance has made any kind of inroad.

You will also have observed that *Time's* editors recognize Cardinal Dopfner as the "highest teaching authority." Yet I submit that in the eyes of an omniscient Rev. Wally White, the Cardinal's statements could just as easily be construed as "an assault on established religious doctrines" as any of the tenets contained in the "formal heresy" of reincarnation.

Religious intolerence undergoes an even more penetrating X-ray examination than the one administered by Cardinal Dopfner in this brief precept by the Jewish essayist Harry Golden.

"Perhaps, most important of all inspirations," submits Golden, "the anti-Semite often burns with a consuming hatred of Jesus, which he prudently expresses against the people who produced Him.

"Hating Jews also allows the anti-Semite to strike blows against the restraining ethics of Christianity without risking his standing in the community."

In short, the narcotic euphoria of false righteousness inevitably leads to persecution.

Persecution must invariably enforce retaliation, no matter how pathetic or ineffectual, even in the forsaken echelons of sexual inversion, where the homosexual is rated as a monster rather than a glandular cripple. Shorn of social rights and privileges, he has inherited the cloak of the outcast pariah which was worn, in the last century, by the immigrants fleeing the European despots and ghettos.

A hundred years ago, signs in office windows informed the unemployed that "Irishmen and Dogs Need Not Apply." The Jew found himself as isolated in his segregated quarter of New York as he had been in Warsaw or Prague. The Negro was reduced to the bondage of the humanoids in Atlantis. This brave new race of free men, for all its unique birthright, still simmered in the melting pot; it was still polyglot; and even now the true indigenous American "conceived in liberty" has yet to emerge.

But *will* he; until all intolerance has vanished from the fifty states?

Cayce, in his self-imposed hypnosis, says no. This nation stuck its chin out as no nation had ever done, when it wrote its Constitution—as literal a covenant with God as any in the Bible. Other nations, not committed as this one is, do not have to achieve or sustain such idealistic standards, even though half Europe and most of Asia still adhere to cynical and obsolete manifestos that deny man's right to "equality, brotherhood and liberty."

Reincarnation reiterates in every tenet, theme and credo that a mock religion creates a mock people— that the root of all evil, the lethal poison man still feeds himself, is the sly and shameful hankering to persecute without being caught at it.

CHAPTER EIGHTEEN

REINCARNATION IN THE FUTURE

In the material world, coming events always cast their shadow, even if these are discernible only to the hindsight of the historian.

Edgar Cayce was always reluctant to force his theories on others, but in the speeches he made to the people at the Cayce Hospital in the early thirties, he indicated his own beliefs of what lay ahead. He saw a development in man's faculties, a broadening of his five senses, and, by implication, a rational and logical acceptance of deeper truths.

If reincarnation lies inherent in these deeper truths, it will be automatically recognized and accepted by the human race as they attain to that plateau of deeper perception.

Cayce himself was already able to read minds and see auras, and described his reactions in these simple words: "Ever since I can remember, I have seen colors in connection with people. I do not remember a time when the human beings I encountered did not register on my retina with blues and greens and reds gently pouring from their heads and shoulders. It was a long time before I realized that other people did not see these colors; it was a long time before I heard the word 'aura,' and learned to apply it to a phenomenon which to me had always been commonplace.

"I never think of people except in connection with their auras; I see them change in my friends and loved ones as time goes by—by sickness, dejection, love, fulfillment. For me, the aura is the weathervane of the soul. It shows which way the winds of destiny are blowing.

"Many people have had experiences similar to mine, not knowing for many years that it was something unique.

"I have heard many people comment on the prevalence of eyeglasses among our civilized peoples. They seem to consider this a bad thing. Could it be that it is a result of constant straining on the part of our eyes to see more, and to bring us to the next step of evolution? I think this is true, and will be accepted in the future.

"What will it mean to us if we make this next evolutionary step? Well, it will mean that all of us will be able to see auras.

"An aura is an effect, not a cause. Every atom, every molecule, every group of atoms and molecules, however simple or complex, tells the story of itself —its pattern, its purpose—through the vibrations which emanate from it.

"As the soul of an individual travels through the realms of being, it shifts and changes its pattern as it uses or abuses the opportunities presented to it. The human eye perceives these vibrations as colors.

"Thus at any time, in any world, a soul will radiate its history through its vibrations. If another consciousness can apprehend those vibrations and understand them, it will know the state of its fellow-soul, the plight he is in, or the progress he has made.

"Imagine what that will mean! Everyone will be able to see when you plan to tell them a lie, even a little white one! We will all have to be frank, for there will no longer be such a thing as deceit!

"Danger, catastrophe, accidents, death, will not come unannounced. We will see them on their way, as did the prophets of old; and, as the prophets of old, we will recognize and welcome our own death, understanding its true significance.

"It is difficult to project ourselves into such a world—a world where people will see each other's faults and virtues, their weaknesses and strength, their sickness, their misfortunes, their coming success. We will see ourselves as others see us, and we will be an entirely different race of people. How many of our vices will persist, when all of them are known to everyone?"

In similar vein, he explained his attitude to the latent power of mental concentration, which is also due to increase in the human race.

"My experience has taught me that practically every phase of phenomena may be explained by the activities of the subconscious mind. First, let me tell you one of my own experiments along these lines— an experiment I have never repeated! In telling you why, I can give you my ideas as to how mental telepathy should and should not be used.

"Many years ago, when I was operating a photographic studio, a young lady who was really a musician was working in my studio. She had become interested in photography and in the phenomena which manifested through me.

"One day I told her that I could force an individual to come to me. I said this because I had been thinking about the subject and studying it. I believed that by deep concentration one should be able to hold a mental image within oneself, and by 'seeing' another

person doing a thing, one could mentally induce tha
person to do it.

"The young lady said, 'Well, I believe most of the
things you've told me, but this is one thing I do no
believe! You'll certainly have to prove it to me!'

"'All right,' I said. 'Who are two people you con
sider it would be impossible for me to influence?'

"'You couldn't get my brother to come up here,
she said, 'and I know you couldn't get Mr. B to
come here either, because he dislikes you.'

"I told her that before twelve o'clock the next day
her brother would not only come up to the studio
but he would ask me to do something for him. 'And
the next day, before two o'clock,' I told her, 'Mr. B
will come here.'

"She shook her head, and said that she couldn'
believe anything of the kind.

"Now our studio was so arranged that from the
second floor we could look into a mirror and see
what was going on in the street below. At ten o'clock
the next day, I sat in meditation for about thirty
minutes, just thinking about her brother and wonder
ing if perhaps I hadn't overstepped myself in saying
he was going to ask me to do something for him
because his sister often told me that he had no
patience with the work I did.

"After about half an hour of this concentrated
thought, I saw the boy pass on the street below, then
turn and come to the steps. He stood there a few
seconds, looking up the steps—then walked away
In a few minutes he returned and came up the stair
to the second floor.

"His sister looked around and exclaimed, 'Wha
are you doing here?'

"The boy sat on the edge of the table, turning hi
hat around in his hands. Then he said, 'Well, I
hardly know—but I had some trouble last night a

266

he shop, and you've been talking so much about Mr. Cayce, I just wondered if he couldn't help me out.'

"His sister almost fainted!

"The next day, at eleven o'clock, I took my seat in the same chair. The girl said, 'If you worked it on my brother, I guess you can work it on Mr. B!'

"I told her I preferred not to be there when Mr. B came, because he disliked me so much, and that he wouldn't know why he had come. She told me afterwards that he came in about twelve-thirty, after I had gone out. She asked him if she could do anything for him. He said, 'No. I don't know what I'm doing here!' and walked out!

"But as I studied these matters more and more, I decided never to do such a thing again. Anyone who wants to control another person, can do it—but beware! The very thing you wish to control in the other person will be the thing that will destroy you. It will become your Frankenstein!

"For, as the information of the Readings say, anyone who would force another to submit to his will is a tyrant. Even God does not force His will upon us. Either we make our will one with His, or we are opposed to Him. Each person has an individual choice.

"Then what part may mental telepathy play in our lives? For anything good can also be dangerous. I could mention nothing good that does not also have its misapplication, its misuse. How, then, may we use mind reading, or mental telepathy, constructively?

"The best rule I can give is this: don't ask another person to do anything you would not do yourself.

"When the Master went down into Judea, He was asked by one of the noblemen of the district, a Pharisee, to have dinner with him.

"So Jesus accepted this invitation, and His disciples went with Him. As they sat at the table, a woman of the streets came in and washed His feet with her tears and wiped them with the hair of her head. She also anointed His feet with precious ointment.

"The nobleman thought to himself—as many of us would today—'What kind of man is this? Doesn't he know the sort of person she is?' Jesus, knowing what was in his mind, said, 'Simon, I have somewhat to say unto thee. . . . There was a certain creditor which had two debtors; the one owed five hundred pence and the other fifty. And when they had nothing to pay, he frankly forgave them both. Tell me, therefore which of them will love him most? Simon answered and said, 'I suppose that one to whom he forgave most.' And He said unto him, 'Thou hast rightly judged.' (Luke 7:36-50)

"Note that Jesus did not say to Simon, 'This is what you are thinking about,' nor accuse him of being discourteous in not having provided water for His feet, nor oil to anoint His head. Jesus simply spoke in such a way as to awaken in Simon the realization that he should not find fault with another.

"At times, we, too, are able to sense what people are thinking, and we may know the trend their thoughts are taking. At such times, our conversation and actions towards them can only be to show—even as the Master showed Simon—that the inmost thoughts can be known to those who are closely associated with the Divine.

"Those of you who have studied something of the history of Atlantis (in the Readings) know that such forces as mental telepathy were highly developed there. Numbers of people were able to think with such concentration that they could bring material things into existence by the very power of their

268

will. To use such forces for selfish purposes, as they used them, can result only in destruction.

"That same force of mind still exists, just as it did in ancient Atlantis.

"The greatest sins in the world today are still selfishness and the domination of one individual will by another will.

"Few people allow other individuals to live their own lives. We want to tell them how; we want to force them to live our way and see things as we see them. Most wives want to tell their husbands what to do, and most husbands want to tell their wives what they can and cannot do!

"Have you ever stopped to think that no one else answers to God for you? Nor do you answer to God for others.

"If a person will seek first to know himself, then the ability to know another's mind will come. Most of those who will practice it for just a little while can develop along this line. But be sure you don't attempt to do God's work! Be content to do your own, and you'll have your hands full!

"We have a right to tell people our own personal experiences and let them decide for themselves, but not to force them, for God calls upon every man, everywhere, to look, to heed, to understand for himself.

"The answer comes to each one of us, as to whether these abilities are worth developing or not. If we have the proper conception of what 'psychic' means, then we know it is a faculty which exists—has always existed—and is ours by birthright, because we are the sons and daughters of God. We have the ability to make association with the Spirit. For 'God is Spirit and seeks such to worship Him.' (John 4:23)

"When we use the forces within to serve the Creative Forces and God, then we are using them correctly. If we use them for our own selfish interests, they are being abused. Then we become even as the Son of Perdition—call him whatever we will."

And once, when Edgar Cayce was in self-hypnosis, he was asked: "How should we present the work of the A.R.E. to one of orthodox faith?"

"Invite them to come and see," he answered. "Not by imposing, not by impelling. For only those who are in need of answers to 'something within' will heed.

"Do not disturb them, do not find fault. For if thy Father, God, had found fault with every idle word or every unkind act in thine experience, what opportunity would ye have had in this experience?

"If you would know mercy before Him, be merciful and kind to those of whatever faith or group ye may find."

CHAPTER NINETEEN

CONCLUSION

Reincarnation, then, is not a theory; it is a practical code of ethics directly affecting human morality.

It was an essential part of the early Gospels, and its removal by two macabre pagans has never been satisfactorily accounted for. Scattered references to it still exist in the Bible, but the encyclopedias have been steadily diminishing their emphasis on it since as far back as 1911—the last edition of the *Encyclopedia Britannica* to deal frankly with it under the heading of Metempsychosis.

Edgar Cayce's Readings accept it unequivocally, and repeatedly insist that positive and negative conduct in earlier lives actively affect behavior patterns in the present. That which is negative can be resolved and overcome, once a man is prepared to accept his problems as being entirely of his own making, and therefore responsive to his un-making.

Nowhere does it seem to have been dangerous or harmful to man's spiritual or philosophic beliefs, save when it conflicts with an inflated vanity, or an ego which has become the tail that wags the dog.

Yet no belief has been so stubbornly denied the

benefit of the doubt at the parochial level; never more loudly have its detractors clamored for "proof." But on whose shoulders should the onus of proof rightly lie?

There is no historic proof that Atlantis ever existed. But five hundred years ago there was no historic proof that America ever existed. For that matter there was no historic proof that the Dead Sea Scrolls ever existed until they were discovered by an Arab goatherd by a one-in-a-million chance.

On nearly every subject under the sun, most men will believe almost any lie—provided it is big enough, absurd enough and is repeated often enough—and never dream of demanding proof. Likewise he will believe what he reads in the papers, and what he sees on the newscasts, as implicitly as if Moses had brought them down Mount Sinai engraved on stone. He will totally accept the election promises of a demagogue. He is blindly convinced that his lawyer, his doctor and his dentist are infallible and incorruptible. If his doctor operates for appendicitis and inadvertently leaves a gauze pad behind when he sews him up, he will obligingly die before he demands to know why the operation had not been as successful as it was cracked up to be.

Apparently only reincarnation fills him with the superstitious dread, and only when he is plagued by dread as vague as that does he insist on proof so irrefutable that not even the Mother of All Living could supply it to his satisfaction.

Why is the karmic law of rebirth and restitution such a scapegoat for the orthodox mind? Is it the fact that every soul in creation will have to voluntarily return and experience the emotional equivalent, good and bad, of all that he has caused others to experience? The fact that whatever weakness we persecute in others we shall eventually inherit, with all its attendant persecution.

The fact that each soul is its own judge and its own jury, and passes sentence only on itself.

The fact that the hereafter shelters no bribable judge, no jury to be bamboozled.

The fact that in the last analysis, the only person anyone has ever kidded was himself—and unsuccessfully at that.

Our obsessive preoccupation with external superficialities, and our servile anxiety to conform to the modern not only rob us of individuality and stature, they corrode us until we become complacent and stultified. Is it only because we have rejected the law of reincarnation that we squander three quarters of our lives, impressing others, pretending to be what we are not? If so, there will have to come a time when we find it almost impossible to be honest with ourselves; and by then nothing will be more painfully and desperately necessary to our sanity.

Perhaps the unpalatable ingredient lies in the fact that, even when it is reduced to its humblest factors, reincarnation offers little if any consolation to the indolent neurotic who blames his blowsy mom and boozy dad for the fact that he has never taken the slightest trouble to make himself likable—let alone lovable—to others. It has no panacea to offer the drone who sullenly sits and waits to be loved for all his faults—for his shiftlessness, his goldbricking, his pharisaic buck-passing, and his furtive longing to play the bully-boy without being made to pay the piper for it.

"So oft is the ego so enrapt in self," Edgar Cayce said, "that it constantly fears it will lose its importance, its place, its freedom. Yet to have freedom in self, give it! To have peace in self, make it! These are immutable laws. . . . For in patience possess ye your souls. In patience you become aware that the body is but a temple, an outward edifice. But the mind and the soul are the permanent furnishings thereof—the essentials in which you shall constantly abide."

This certainly clashes with the fine old materialistic maxim that the world hates a loser and admires a self-made big shot, no matter how many victims he leaves in his wake.

Have we, by discarding the law of reincarnation, discarded all concept of a just and loving Creator? Then we would seem to have created our own booby traps with a vengeance. For surely man's five senses are insufficient to enable him to deny the existence of God with any real conviction.

Isn't man on safer ground accepting rather than denying Him? For once he succeeds in reducing all belief to nothing, he himself, obviously, no longer exists.

This would seem to indicate that a professed atheist is only a man who cannot contemplate the firmament without getting vertigo, because it offers him nothing familiar to compare it against.

Perhaps this explains why he has equal difficulty trying to comtemplate the idea of reincarnation. The idea that it is one of the logical cornerstones of a valid faith lacks a comforting solid, materialistic base. This fact alone is enough to make it suspect to any self-condemned penitent who believes that he was born in sin once and once only, and that the only way to his own conception of a bedraggled salvation is through senseless and interminable suffering.

To him, the abiding heresy of reincarnation is that man is a free agent and his God is a God of Love. This means that until he has learned to love his fellow men, no further knowledge of his Maker is available to him.

What confronts him next? The unpalatable fact that no man is capable of loving others until he has overcome the obstacles which prevent him from loving himself.

If he can never love or become lovable to others, it follows as logically as day follows night that others can never love or become lovable to him.

In which case, he is now in sore and mortal trouble, for if he can neither love nor be loved, he will be engulfed by the eternal night of implacable loneliness. Loneliness is man's most lethal adversary, for it is the only poison which can ultimately and inexorably exterminate the soul.

The reader who has realized by now that any serious study of reincarnation can not be approached through any other channel than the dependence on a benign Christ, will do well to de-dogmatize himself by resorting to the Rev. Weatherhead's beautifully conceived and simply written *The Christian Agnostic* (Abingdon Press, New York, 1965). No other cleric of such estimable authority has ever been more in harmony with Edgar Cayce's own interpretation of the Bible.

In the chapter *"Reincarnation and Renewed Chances,"* Dr. Weatherhead spearheads his own acceptance of metempsychosis in the following words: "I think of Betty Smith, born into a prosperous home, surrounded by every opportunity, given an ideal education, loving and marrying a man well able to keep her in the same kind of environment, giving life to half a dozen happy, healthy children, and passing into middle and later life with full health and every possible amenity.

"Then I think of Jane Jones, born blind, or deaf, or crippled, into a poverty-stricken home, where a drunken father makes life a hell for everyone. Jane cannot escape, can never marry and have her own home, can never be given the things Betty enjoys, and dies early, let us say, of malignant disease. . . .

"Some imagine that 'things will be squared up in heaven.'

"Is Betty, then, to suffer in another life because she was happy on earth? What would that do, in the matter of justice? Nothing. And certainly it would do Jane no good. Nor is she vindictive or mean enough to desire it. Is Jane to be 'rewarded' or 'compensated?'

"But what kind of compensation makes up for half a century of earthly misery? We cringe when we hear of a grant of money given to a man wrongfully imprisoned. How can that make up to him for the mental distress, the wasted years, the misery and pain to all his relatives? These things cannot be 'made-up' for.

"Is human distress just luck, then? If so, how un just is life! Is it God's will? Then how unlike any human father he must be; for a human father who thus exerted his will would be clapped into jail, or into a lunatic asylum!"

These are strong words from the august Minister of London's City Temple, but Dr. Weatherhead hits as hard as Cayce ever did. Dr. Weatherhead be lieves passionately that Christianity is a way of life not "a theological system with which one must be in intellectual agreement. . . ."

"If you love Christ and are seeking to follow him take an attitude of Christian agnosticism to intel lectual problems, at least for the present. . . .

"Frankly I often wonder why so many people do go to church. Christianity must have a marvellous in herent power, or the churches would have killed it long ago."

Even so, reincarnation will be allotted no logical place in our society until orthodox dogma ceases to cater to (and thus only attract) the guilt-ridden factor in its congregations. Reincarnation can never make sense to the man in the street as long as he secretly fears and rejects his obsolete concept of a vindictive and avenging God.

Dr. Weatherhead, as Cayce did before him, makes this the cornerstone of his whole argument, and he takes particular exception to an English cleric who, having used every specious bromide to discredit metempsychosis, ended with the defiant: "My alleged pre-existence can have no present moral meaning simply because I am debarred from remembering anything about it."

Here the well-intentioned worthy led with his chin, and Dr. Weatherhead was cheerfully in his rights to tap him on it.

"What a preposterous statement!" Dr. Weatherhead exclaims. "So if some drug were now given to Dr. Whale, blotting out the memory of his youth, any indiscretions of that youth could have 'no present moral meaning!' He forgets that they would just as effectively have made him and molded him to be what he is, as if he remembered them. A judge is not often ready to excuse a prisoner of all moral responsibility if he asserts that he can't remember anything about it now!

"None of us can now remember his earliest years. But any psychologist will stress their importance and the effect they had upon us.

"These childhood incidents happened, not to another, but to us, and, though now forgotten, determined many of our present reactions to life. The very pattern of adult life is a form of stored memory. We do not need to remember mental impressions to be influenced by them."

And in the same mood of amiable exuberance, Dr. Weatherhead presents this straightforward argument: "The intelligent Christian believes that God is working out a plan in the lives of all men and women, and that the consummation of this plan will mean that his will is 'done on earth as it is in heaven' . . .

"(But) how can a world progress in inner things —which are the most important—if the birth of every new generation fills the world with unregenerate souls full of untamed, animal tendencies? There can never be a perfect world unless, gradually, those born into it can take advantage of lessons learned in earlier lives instead of starting at scratch. True, the number of prodigies is small and so is the number of saints, but there may well be other planets more adequate than this is, to be their classroom. It may be that we must relinquish the idea of this earth being the venue of the perfect society.

"These thoughts make me agree with the late Dean Inge, no mean thinker, who said of the doctrine or reincarnation, 'I find it both credible and attractive.'

"One wonders why men have so readily accepted the idea of a life after death and so largely, in the West, discarded the idea of a life before birth. So many arguments for a one-way immortality seem to me cogent for a two-way life outside the present body."

But even if we confine the issue to life after death, we can do no better than conclude with one of Edgar Cayce's favorite parables from the Bible.

In Luke 17:19-31, Christ tells the Pharisees of the beggar Lazarus, "fed from the crumbs of the rich man's table," who died and was taken to Abraham's bosom. But when the rich man died, he found himself in hell, from which vantage point he could see Lazarus ensconced in Heaven.

"Then he said (to Abraham), "I pray thee therefore, father, than thou would send him to my father's house; for I have five brethren; that he may testify unto them, lest they also come into this place of torment."

"Abraham said to him, 'They have Moses and the prophets. Let them hear them.'

"And (the rich man) said, 'Nay, father Abraham: but if one went unto them from the dead, they will repent.'

"And Abraham said unto him, 'If they hear not Moses and the prophets, neither will they be persuaded, though one rose from the dead.'"

RECOMMENDED PARALLEL READING

Books:
TWENTY CASES SUGGESTIVE OF REINCAR-
NATION by Ian Stevenson, M.D.
MANY MANSIONS by Gina Cerminara, Ph.D.
THE WORLD WITHIN by Gina Cerminara, Ph.D.
REINCARNATION: AN EAST-WEST ANTHOLO-
GY by Joseph Head and S. L. Cranston

Pamphlets:
THE CASE FOR REINCARNATION by Leslie D.
Weatherhead
THE EVIDENCE FOR SURVIVAL FROM
CLAIMED MEMORIES OF FORMER INCAR-
NATIONS by Ian Stevenson, M.D.

APPENDIX

THE FIFTEEN ANATHEMAS AGAINST ORIGEN

Henry Percival has printed in full the fifteen anathemas against Origen. They are easily available in Head and Cranston's admirable *Reincarnation, An East-West Anthology* (The Julian Press, New York, 1961) and seldom have such grandiose dictums carried such disproportionate substance. Indeed, they read more like illiterate bombast than responsibly conceived tenets, and literally nowhere do they quote Biblical authority for their condemnations.

"If anyone assert the fabulous pre-existence of souls", they begin grandiloquently, "and shall assert the monstrous restoration which follows it, let him be anathema (cursed)."

Clause 2: "If anyone shall say that the creation of all reasonable things includes only intelligences without bodies . . . and that there is unity between them all by identity of substance, force and energy, and by their union with and knowledge of God the Word; but that, no longer desiring the sight of God, they gave themselves over to worse things, each one following his own inclination; and that they have taken

281

bodies more or less subtle, and have received name
. . . let him be anathema."

(This would suggest an impeachment of the entire
Bible, for even the Old Testament states that all
living things were originally conceived in the mind
of God, were given Entity by Him, and subsequently
rejected their source and their Maker).

Clauses 3 and 5 submerge themselves in their own
unintelligibility, but Clause 7 announces: "If anyone
shall say that Christ . . . had pity upon the divers fall
which had appeared in the spirits . . . and that to
restore them He passed through divers classes, had
different bodies and different names, became all to
all, an Angel among Angels, a Power among Powers
. . . and finally has taken flesh and blood like our
and is become man for man. . . . if anyone says all
this and does not profess that God the Word humbled
himself and became man; let him be anathema."

(The unabbreviated text is even more labored in
its effort to discredit Christ's incarnation in a human
form; and yet it tries to imply at the same time that
He might have done something vaguely similar, but
too obscurely to be intelligible to mortal reason. This
is typical of Theodora's constant anxiety-neurosis to
have her cake and obliterate it too.)

Clause 8 is an even more complex non sequitur:
"If anyone shall not acknowledge that God the
Word . . . is Christ in every sense of the word, but
shall affirm that He is so only in an inaccurate manner and because of the abasement of the intelligence
and *e converso* that the intelligence is only called God
because of the Logos, let him be anathema."

(If any sense can be got out of this, it surely entirely discredits Christ's own affirmation that he was
both the Son of God and the Son of Man.)

Clauses 9 and 10 and 11 entangle themselves in
each other's verbiage to such an extent as to cancel

out their combined rodomontade; but Clause 12 makes an effort to salvage the best of the preceding clauses: "If anyone shall say that the future judgment signifies the destruction of the body; and that . . . thereafter there will no longer be any matter, but only spirit, let him be anathema."

(This makes Christ's symbolic triumph over the flesh by His death and resurrection a pointless gesture, performed for absolutely no constructive purpose whatsoever.)

Clause 14 blunders even more unwittingly into passive atheism: "If anyone shall say that all reasonable beings will one day be united in one . . . and the bodies shall have disappeared, and that the knowledge of the world to come will carry with it the ruin of worlds . . . that in this pretended apocatastasis, spirits only will continue to exist, as it was in the feigned pre-existence; let him be anathema."

(In short, "all this shall not pass away.")

Clause 15: "If anyone shall say that the life of the Spirits shall be like to the life which was in the beginning, when as yet the spirits had not come down or fallen; so that the end . . . shall be the true measure of the beginning; let him be anathema."

Small wonder that even the intimidated Pope Virgilius moved heaven and earth to get such claptrap anathematized in its own turn; and that Justinian had to resort to a Byzantine filibuster to railroad it through.

But there was yet more idiocy to come.

In his auto-intoxication (for by now the whole process of creation must have seemed as clear as mud to the self-apotheosized Justinian), he personally contributed ten more gratuitous anathemas against Origen.

These are even more deranged in content than the first fifteen, except that two of the clauses are direct attacks on church concepts which even predate Origen. The first relates to the idea of Christ descending to purgatory and submitting to a form of crucifixion there, as the only means of redeeming the souls of the damned. (Reference to this appears often enough in the early church writings to establish that it must at one time have held an honored place in the Gospels.)

"If anyone says or thinks that Christ the Lord in a future time will be crucified for demons, as he was for man, let him be anathema," trumpets Justinian, gorgeously impervious to the possibility that he and his formidable spouse might one day languish among those selfsame demons, in abiding need of salvation from the Son of Man.

The next point lies even further back in antiquity—the poetic concept of the soul, once it is free of its material confines, as a luminous glow of pure light. It was one of Origen's pet images, and Justinian skewers it grimly: "If anyone says or thinks that at the resurrection, human bodies will rise spherical in form and unlike our present forms, let him be anathema."

(Here one senses the outraged Theodora refusing to conceive of herself on Judgment Day as anything less spherical than a heavily bejeweled Empress, diplomatic immunity intact.)

The last of the ten clauses is the most petulant:

"If anyone says or thinks that the punishment of demons and of impious men is only temporary, and will one day have to end, and that a restoration will take place of demons and impious men, let him be anathema."

(So you can forget the parable of the Prodigal Son.)

THE A.R.E. TODAY

The Association for Research and Enlightenment, Inc., is a non-profit, open membership organization committed to spiritual growth, holistic healing, psychical research and its spiritual dimensions; and more specifically, to making practical use of the psychic readings of the late Edgar Cayce. Through nationwide programs, publications and study groups, A.R.E. offers all those interested, practical information and approaches for individual study and application to better understand and relate to themselves, to other people and to the universe. A.R.E. membership and outreach is concentrated in the United States with growing involvement throughout the world.

The headquarters at Virginia Beach, Virginia,

includes a library/conference center, administrative offices and publishing facilities, and are served by a beachfront motel. The library is one of the largest metaphysical, parapsychological libraries in the country. A.R.E. operates a bookstore, which also offers mail-order service and carries approximately 1,000 titles on nearly every subject related to spiritual growth, world religions, parapsychology and transpersonal psychology. A.R.E. serves its members through nationwide lecture programs, publications, a Braille library, a camp and an extensive Study Group Program.

The A.R.E. facilities, located at 67th Street and Atlantic Avenue, are open year-round. Visitors are always welcome and may write A.R.E., P.O. Box 595, Virginia Beach, VA 23451, for more information about the Association.

For all U.K. general inquiries, newsletter and study group information contact:

Edgar Cayce Centre
P.O. Box 8
Stanley
County Durham
DH9 7XQ

Of further interest . . .

EDGAR CAYCE ON ESP

The secrets of the paranormal world —
and how to use them yourself

DORIS AGEE
Edited by HUGH LYNN CAYCE

Edgar Cayce On ESP is the definitive work on this celebrated prophet's extraordinary achievements in parapsychological phenomena. Anyone who has ever been intrigued by the paranormal will be fascinated by this book, which opens up a bewildering area of human ESP capacities. The remarkable topics covered include out-of-body travel, clairvoyance, auras, telepathy, precognition, dreams, and personal psychic development.

The late Edgar Cayce's groundbreaking psychic perception in the areas of healing, dreams, nutrition, health, reincarnation, religion — and extra-sensory perception — have made him the most respected clairvoyant of our time. *Edgar Cayce On ESP* was edited by Hugh Lynn Cayce, Mr Cayce's son and former director of the Association for Research and Enlightenment, an organization dedicated to the practical employment of his father's psychic findings.

EDGAR CAYCE ON DREAMS

**True-life examples of dream interpretation —
and how to make it work for you**

DR HARMON H BRO
Edited by HUGH LYNN CAYCE

Edgar Cayce On Dreams reveals Cayce's revolutionary
psychic perceptions on what dreams mean and how to
interpret them. 'In dreams, people experience for
themselves every important kind of psychic phenomenon,
and every level of helpful psychological and religious
counsel', he said. In this fascinating book, astonishing case
histories demonstrate how you can bring conscious insight
into dreaming that will awaken new possibilities in your life.

The late Edgar Cayce's psychic achievements in healing,
ESP, nutrition, health, reincarnation, religion — and
dreams — have made him the most respected clairvoyant
of our time. Dr Harmon Bro, author of *Edgar Cayce On
Dreams,* is the only trained social scientist to have studied
Edgar Cayce in person. Editor Hugh Lynn Cayce was Mr
Cayce's son and former director of the Association for
Research and Enlightenment, an organization dedicated
to the practical employment of his father's psychic
findings.